"Just a Little Rain..."

...Baby Boomers & Military Brats Reflect
on Childhood, Baseball, and War...

A memoir of men and one amazing woman,
growing up in the 1950s & 1960s around the world

Bob Flournoy
& A Few Friends

PublishAmerica
Baltimore

© 2005 by Bob Flournoy.
All rights reserved. No part of this book may be reproduced, stored in a retrieval system or transmitted in any form or by any means without the prior written permission of the publishers, except by a reviewer who may quote brief passages in a review to be printed in a newspaper, magazine or journal.

First printing

ISBN: 1-4137-5391-4
PUBLISHED BY PUBLISHAMERICA, LLLP
www.publishamerica.com
Baltimore

Printed in the United States of America

For all the moms who washed our clothes and watched us play, and wound up watching the mail box and waiting for the phone to ring.

Maude Cobb Flournoy
1924 - 1990

Thanks, Mom.
You were always there, quietly, lovingly, patiently.
We miss you every day

Thanks, guys, for contributing with such gusto and literate passion when first baited to be a part of this project, and for 45 years of friendship.

Robert W. Flournoy, Jr. (Dad) is a retired army officer living in Cape Coral, Florida.

Mike Day is an independent film producer in the Wahsington D.C. area.

Mike King is a director ITT Sciences in Colorado Springs.

Joe Gelineau is a division manager for Siemens in Orlando.

Sharon Larrison is a senior sales executive for Novartis in Atlanta.

Ray Hill is a professor of economics at Emory University in Atlanta.

Jack Hopke is in the radio industry in New Orleans.

Mike Marotta works for Columbia HCA in Nashville, where he also coaches high school hockey.

Ed Condon is retired from Pharmacia and is a college instructor and wood artist.

Paul Cowan produces radio shows for the music industry in Nashville.

Special thanks to Southern Cultures *magazine for publishing my first essay* "A Southern Memory," *Spring 2004, most of which appears in this book.*

A Lull Between Storms

Bob Flournoy

We were the original baby boomers. We loved the air raid drills that broke up a school day's monotony, and we chased the milkman on our bikes, hoping for a chunk of ice on a hot summer day. A nickel in our pockets as we awaited the tinkling bell of the popsicle man was all that we needed to make our day, unless we were fortunate enough to have a dime for a nutty buddy. Born in the mid 1940s, we entered the post war world with the exploits of our fathers as shining beacons of duty and courage to light our ways. Many of us were in military families who traveled the world and caught what glimpses we could of normal hometown childhood.

For some, this was a good experience. For others, it was not. Although our childhood memories may vary with geography and family culture, boys of my generation seem to have some things in common that are universal, regardless of social status, or where we grew up. Those *things* were sports in general, baseball in particular, and we played *army*. Boys and girls who were born after the Korean War, as a general rule, do not have those sepia toned snapshots burned into that special part of their brains that retain the black and white memories of an era that made us different. They entered a Technicolor world that had outgrown radio in favor of television, a brand new world that was beginning to share America's baseball monopoly with other sports, right there in full color for the asking, without the need or necessity to play outdoors all day long in the fresh air and sun.

They also found themselves on T-ball teams in full uniform at age five, and played and even practiced in front of cheering white collar parents who had lifestyles more relaxed than our own hard-working parents had, and that afforded them this new-found leisure time to spend with their children. Nope, an era died when kids my age grew up, and few since have known the sweet satisfaction of sitting on a dark porch on a soft summer evening with their dads, often their whole families, and listening to the lost art of live-action-radio sports-broadcasting. Without the visual aids of television, commentators, many of whom were as popular as the players, painted a picture for us with their colorful descriptive banter, as clear and beautiful as if we were there in person.

In fact, I knew exactly what to expect when I attended my first major league game. The scene before me at ten years old was a duplicate of what I had been watching on the radio for many years. In this case, it was an exhibition game in El Paso, Texas, between the Giants and the Indians in March of 1958. Little did I know that I was witnessing the beginning of the great betrayal, as this was the first game ever where a major league team had made a move and was representing a new town, a new city, and new fans. It was also the year of the much celebrated overtime and televised National Football League game that elevated football to the same interest level as baseball, feeding the growing appetite of the American public for something more violent in what would become larger, rowdier arenas.

The lure of big money had given California two storied east coast teams at a cost to the game that would not be felt for several more years, but would forever change the flavor of our favorite past-time. Many of you will remember when I tell you that Willie Mays was young and in his prime and Herb Score was trying to stage a come back after being almost killed by a Gil McDougal line drive into his face the year before. What else could you expect from a damn

Yankee, whom we loved to hate, despite having a line-up in the late '50s that every single boy in the USA could name whether he liked them or not. Skowron, Kubek, Mantle, Maris… Gods, all of them. I was absolutely speechless at the speed of Score's fastball. Flabbergasted. Scared that I would ever in my life have to face something like that, I began to doubt my future in the game, but reveled in the atmosphere and just being a part of the crowd where people yelled, "Hey, Willie, can you come over here and sign my boy's ball?" And he did, with a smile that challenged the blinding desert sun in that local ball park.

I had a hot dog that day, of course, and carried my glove with me the entire time. I was to realize later, that also in that ball park were Bob Feller, Early Winn and Bob Lemon. Curiously, as I watched that game in person, live, for the first time, I was listening to a voice on the radio describe every move on the diamond. I can hear myself to this day. There are ten million memories. No, a hundred million, in the heads of men who grew up with me and before I was born. Even if you were not good enough to play when you got older, the field was pretty level before you were eleven or twelve, and you were out there with the boys, in the sun, every day, playing baseball.

These accounts are the memories of men, and one remarkable woman, who were kids in the '50s and would come of age in the tumultuous '60s, witnessing assassinations of our country's leaders, a nation ripped apart by racial strife, and a decade of war in which so many would participate, willingly, shadowing the feats of our fathers, not to mention John Wayne. And, although the magic of our youth came to a sudden halt all too soon, baseball, and a sense of duty, since obscured by the noise of a new landscape, ran in our veins when we were young.

El Paso, Texas

Bob Flournoy, III

When my father returned from Korea in the summer of 1953, I was six years old. En route to El Paso, Texas, for his next duty assignment, we visited with my grandparents for a week on their south Alabama farm. While there, my grandfather, father, and I wandered one hot day into the cotton fields that surrounded the old farm house. This was always an adventure for me, ever on the lookout for some kind of game animal to make a dash out of the bushes in our path.

Some atavistic instinct was already stirring in me that responded to that kind of setting, which made me aware of nature and the possibilities that it held. I longed to be able to carry my own shotgun into those fields as soon as possible. I knew that I would be a deadly shot, bringing home a bountiful and endless supply of game for the family to feast upon. But, on this day, there were no rabbits to chase or deer to kick their heels in our faces. There was only the loose sandy soil of that cotton field and the heavy humid heat beating down from a pale blue summer southern sky.

In a subconscious, weary gesture, my granddad stooped over and picked up a handful of drought-dried dirt and let it run in a fine powder slowly through his fingers back to the ground. With a wistful smile he glanced up and said, in a conversational tone that I can hear like he spoke the words yesterday, "Ah, Lord…give us a little rain; just a little shower will do the trick."

"Amen to that," responded my dad.

I think I glanced up and thought, *fat chance,* as I peered into the cloudless horizon, thinking of the dark walls of water that would often advance across that open expanse around us, bringing a fresh coolness to the parched air of south Alabama in August.

We left Alabama shortly after that walk and headed for Texas and this, I assure you, was anticipated as a real big trip because Texas was where the cowboys and Indians still lived and I thrilled to the landmarks as we passed them. The Red River was brown, the bushes were brown and there was sand, sand, sand. The sand was flat and hard or it formed dunes, and it blew and stung. Alabama did not know dry and I had never seen such uninterrupted sky. But, there was a haunting beauty to that endless country that I was to grow to love, as would my family, without knowing when it actually became a part of us.

Many years later my mother and I watched a movie together, *Tender Mercies,* where an old hung-over cowboy wandered into the desert behind the run down motel he was staying in and surveyed the barren landscape that stretched forever and symbolized the emptiness in his life. Without meaning to, Mom said softly to herself in a whisper, "How beautiful." She was responding to something that had touched her long ago during our time in the southwest, and I heard in her simple words that which had entered my own heart long ago and would keep drawing me back for the rest of my life.

But, in the meantime, as I stared out the window of our little car, I was wondering where the buffalo and teepees were. Little did I know that they awaited me just ahead and that I was about to learn my first lesson in life about how events kind of tie together if you are alert to such things, even as a youngster. So, two days into our trip, somewhere around Van Horn on U.S. Highway 80 in the blazing summer heat of an un-airconditioned car in West Texas, I was dozing on a sweaty pillow in the sweltering back seat. My dad pulled off the road and announced that we were going to take a little break. I looked sleepily out the window and blasted awake and out of the car because we were smack-dab in the middle of a bunch of Indian teepees. *Wow, what was this!?*

It was an Indian reservation, the likes of which still existed in the 1950s, and pretty authentic if memory serves me correctly. At any rate, to a six year old (almost seven!) it was the real deal and I was in it. We wandered around, eating snow cones, me clutching a "genuine" tomahawk that my mom had purchased from a real chief (he must have been, because he had a war bonnet on), and drifted into a small set of wooden bleachers with some other tourists to watch a ceremony that was unfolding before us.

A group of old men had emerged, painted and feathered, and they were chanting and shuffling around in the dry dirt, raising their hands to the sky and stomping up little clouds around their heavy feet as the intensity of their dance increased. When they stopped, they were enveloped in a smoky dust and their faces were raised to the sky. There was a reverence in the air that made everyone stay very quiet. I nudged my dad and asked him in a whisper if we had just witnessed a real war dance. He said no, that we had just seen a timeless prayer, as old as civilization itself, the old grandfathers were asking God for rain.

A Child's Viewpoint

Mike Day

Mike Day, Batboy, 1951

In the beginning there was innocence and then came baseball; perfect timing. By the age of eight, I knew exactly what I wanted to be when I grew up: a saint. A saint who made his living as the greatest baseball player in history. It wouldn't be easy, I knew that. But any saint worthy of the name expects to endure suffering of major league proportions. Why should I be any different? It's true that as the first child of an American father hailing from Brooklyn and a French Catholic mother, born in the rubble of postwar France and raised on U.S. Army bases in occupied Germany, I was a mongrel stew of racial genetics. But this only made me as tough as I was tiny, and is not to be considered a shortcoming or flaw, especially when you consider the general mental and physical health of purebreds, who are, if I'm not mistaken, inbreds.

Anyway, for the sake of dramatic unity, I wish I could say that the tracks of my dual destinies—sainthood and baseball legend—were set into motion on the very same Saturday. In fact, they were. It was probably the most successful day of my life, career-wise: the day I made altar boy before lunch and bat boy by dinner. In the Patrick Henry Village chapel that morning, a handful of us altar-boys-in-training were taking our final exams, proving our ability to mispronounce Latin phrases and knowing when to stop pouring wine into the priest's chalice (some priests liked more water than wine, some liked them in equal measures, a few liked to get the party started). Suddenly, out of nowhere, a loud squawk echoed off an adjoining building and pierced the stucco walls of the chapel, shaking the stained glass windows.

"Testing one, two. SQUAWK..."

I thought my ears would bleed. We were looking at each other for an explanation when the second and third squawk hit.

"SQUAWKING one, SQUAWK three..."

The noise seemed to be coming in from some other dimension. The priest promptly declared that we'd all passed the final exam and earned our cassocks and incense. He assured us that from then on, whenever we served Mass, we would be closer to God than anyone else in the congregation, except for him. Then he followed us outside to see what was going on. There, across the railroad tracks on a large field in the distance, men dressed in pure white uniforms and bright red caps were playing a game with a little white ball and a stick. That's how you'd describe the facts of it. But the reality of it was an entirely different matter. This was a vision, pure and simple. It was unlike anything I'd ever seen, as though we'd been granted a peek at Mount Olympus, where creatures of a divine order were playing a sport known only to the gods.

For a child of eight, there is no gap between impulse and action, and I was already half way up Monroe Strasse, heading home, before

I made the connection between what I had just seen and the funny looking outfit my American grandparents had sent me the previous Christmas. How was I to know that it was the uniform of the gods themselves, the pinstripes of the New York Yankees? By the time I figured out how to wear the long navy blue stockings with strange holes, the squawking sounds of the PA system had transformed into audible announcements of names and positions.

A few seconds later, I was crawling through a hole in the fence along the train tracks. I raced faster and faster toward the spectacle, which by now included a military brass band and a growing crowd. The closer I got, the louder the sounds, the greater the excitement. There was a rowdiness to it that I'd never experienced before: solid cracks of bats, cheering and whistling, line drives slamming into leather mitts, the stink of beer. Underneath the bleachers, older boys were scrounging for empty bottles and running them over to a concession stand, collecting ten cents per bottle. This was a skill I took to immediately. To the older kids' chagrin, I cut into their turf. Whenever an adult had to choose between giving their empty bottle to a pimply teenager or to a cute little kid in his Yankee pin stripes, guess who got it? A pile of those coins felt like a pirate's booty in my hands.

On the other side of the backstop some kid was darting back and forth from the dugout to the batter's box, grabbing bats left behind after a hit and running them back to the dugout. I noticed the other team didn't have one of these bat-runners, so I snuck under the stands to the other end of their dugout and waited to be noticed in my Yankee uniform. I knew it wouldn't take long. Adorable children know their power. Sure enough, one of the players spotted me and smiled, pointing me out to the other GI's sitting on the bench. One after another, they laughed. The word spread quickly through the dugout. I was making an impression.

When the tide of attention was sufficiently turned in my direction, I made my stuttering French into English pitch, "Can I be your boy-who-runs-for-bats?"

Eventually, I was brought to the attention of His Gruffness, the Coach. He squinted in my direction, then spit out a substantial tobacco loogie before grunting, "You want to be a bat boy? Are you kidding? Do bears shit in the woods?"

They gave me a tryout. I didn't know a thing about the game but, by the bottom of the ninth, my two fates were fused.

For the rest of the season, I was the bat boy and official mascot for the Coleman Barracks Indians. They took me under their wing and taught me everything about the game: how to throw; how to hold my glove to catch fly balls and how to use my body to trap grounders; how to catch runners in a squeeze play; how to pick them off base; how to play "pepper" with the long, skinny fungo bats.

They also taught me how to curse. "Hey, Junior, cover your ears."

I loved being called Junior. Not Shorty or Pee Wee, but Junior. I especially liked it when Tom called me Junior. For some reason, he spent more time with me than the other GI's. One day he took me aside and I learned why. He asked if I knew Miss Luther. Did I ever! The lovely, stacked Miss Luther was my third grade teacher. What a coincidence he would know her, too. He asked me to say 'hi' to her for him. Okay, I was a kid, but I wasn't brain dead. I'd heard other GI's whistle when Miss Luther's name came up, usually followed by descriptive hand gestures and exclamations. I didn't always understand the colorful words but I knew what was being said, and I instinctively assumed my rightful role as Miss Luther's protector.

It turned out that she didn't necessarily want to be protected. Instead, she enlisted me as her personal little Cupid to carry messages between her and Tom. By the end of the school year, they were engaged; by autumn, Miss Luther returned to school as Mrs. Lee. I never did understand why they hadn't asked me to be an altar boy at their wedding. The concept of different religions was unknown to me back then; otherwise, Miss Luther's very maiden name might have offered a clue to their oversight.

As the summer of '53 slipped into the past, game by game, Junebug by firefly, Mass by Mass, my twin destinies merged nicely. On Sunday afternoons, I dressed up like a priest, tying two towels at my shoulders and served authentic, unblessed Communion wafers which I'd lifted from the sacristy to my two younger sisters, who were acting as altar boys. In my desire to fully replicate the experience, I'd have them pour me some of the Malaga wine that our beloved French "mamama" had given us. Likewise, I brought the authority of my impending sainthood to bear on my sports career by performing ritual blessings on my baseballs and marbles. First, I'd place them in order of size on the windowsill inside my bedroom; then I'd make the Sign of the Cross above them, intoning *"In Nominus Patris et Filius et Spiritus Sanctus"* over my Frenchies, Swissies, Clearies, Steelies, and lowly clay Watchamanuggets. These rituals worked so well it felt like an abuse of divine power.

Meanwhile, I began to recognize some of the players off the field wearing their civvies. They'd show up at the Sullivan Barracks bowling alley where I was a pinboy, arm in arm with their fancy German Frauleins. The women looked kind of hideous to me, but I think I can safely say that the charms of painted ladies require a maturity one must grow into, and I was still processing my third grade teacher. At other times, I'd see the GI's and their Schatzies at the base movie theatre, that temple of dreams, where I religiously snuck in without paying, saving my fifteen cents for a Baby Ruth, JujyFruits, and a large Coke. Inside the theater, before the movie started, the heroic tempos of military marches played like my own personal soundtrack as I scavenged for half-empty bags of popcorn and poured them all into one large bonanza. The extra salt and butter were tasty, but I could do without the uncooked kernels of corn that got stuck in my teeth. I wasn't complaining, though. The popcorn was free.

So were the three or four cartoons and the March of Time newsreels, the ongoing Flash Gordon or whichever serial cliffhangers were out, the four or five coming attractions, and the feature. If it was some B-movie with Richard Widmark, it ran for one day. If it was an A-movie (like *Shane*), it ran for two. The epics, three hours long not counting intermissions—*The Robe* with Victor Mature comes to mind—played for three days before they were replaced by the next movie. The X-movies, of course, were off-limits, though there were times that I'd be watching a movie and I'd hear my mother's voice calling my name in the dark and I'd end up being pulled out through the center aisle by my ear.

We had no television back then, so the movie newsreels provided the only opportunity to see major league baseball players in action. On the other hand, we did have plenty of real-life cursing Army athletes to look up to, some of whom had been former minor league stars back home. And as mascot and batboy, I had a front-row seat to the action, where I watched and learned. It was same at church, where I practiced different pious poses, as if I were rehearsing for beatification. This saint business was going to be easy. All I had to do was stay adorable and prepare to be stoned to death at the hour of God's choosing.

On the baseball diamond, meanwhile, I'd imitate my favorite pitcher's wind-up and delivery, my favorite batter's stance, and my favorite fielder's running underarm fade-away throw to first base. When you're that age, imitation is bone-physical and without thought. Every nerve and fiber of your being responds to the spirit and skill of the game. When the GI games ended, we kids would swarm across the field and make it our own. We'd choose up sides and pick our positions.

I remember the first time I was allowed to pitch, how steep the angle of the pitcher's mound was, and how, when I got to the top, I looked down at the batter like I was king of the mountain. And how far away he looked. And how, when my skinny little arm tried to toss the ball the entire major league distance to home plate, I might as well have been trying to throw the ball to Romania. Still, I practiced every day for hours. I'd throw the ball straight up into the air as high as I could, then try to catch it, glove down. Or I'd pretend to be a pitcher and throw the ball against the side of our apartment building, then quickly switch-pretend into a shortstop just in time to catch the line drive that came back at me. Day after day, every day until dark, I annoyed one and all with the constant th-thump, th-thump, th-thump, that echoed across rows after rows of military housing.

Early the next summer, my father took us to visit his family in America, where they lived perched high among the vast concrete canyons called Manhattan, which had "burrows" around it, and somehow, altogether, they made up New York City. I took my grandparents' word for it. What I couldn't understand was why my father's parents and most of the people in their neighborhood spoke with a German accent. Or why a dead nun was laid out inside a glass altar in the Catholic Church across the street.

At Mass the next morning, my mother whispered to me that the church was named Frances Cabrini and that it was Mother Cabrini herself lying miraculously preserved inside the glass, awaiting her canonization. A little weird. But being a saint-in-progress myself, I took it to mean that I, too, would eventually end up preserved under glass. As the Latin ritual slouched along, the only things keeping me awake were the sight of Mother Cabrini, less than ten feet away, then familiar thumping sounds against one of the walls of the church, and kids yelling. I perked up. This was what I was waiting for.

Adjacent to the church on a concrete lot, surrounded by a high chain-link fence that looked like a cage, American boys with thick New York accents were playing a fast game that resembled baseball; the only difference being they were using a small eraser-pink rubber ball and a long straight stick. I ran over to the fence to watch, hoping they'd invite me to play. But these were older kids and they couldn't care less about some stuttering foreign shrimp. They didn't even see me. So I ran and caught up with my mother at the traffic light and asked her if she had packed my little Yankee uniform.

When the French kid returned to the lot wearing his pinstripes, he was admitted into the inner sanctum, where he was taught the arcane game of stick ball. It was much easier to play than hardball, but the concrete also made it easier to skin your knees to the bloody bone. In between what passed for innings, one of the kids told me about a special day when kids were invited to Yankee Stadium to compete with each other for prizes. All you had to do was write a note to the Yankees and ask.

At lunch, my grandfather said he'd write them a note for me and ask on my behalf. Days later, we got a letter back from the Yankees: my first rejection letter? a form letter, no less? thanking me for my interest and so forth? This had not gone my way. Instead, my father took me to Yankee Stadium to see the Yankees play the Red Sox. We sat in the bleachers and watched Joe Dimaggio play centerfield,

Whitey Ford pitch, and Yogi Berra behind the plate. The stadium was majestic, huge beyond anything I could ever have imagined.

The screams of the New York fans were deafening and they would all rise as one with the crack of every line drive or long ball. They even gave a standing ovation to one of the Red Sox batters: some long, tall, skinny guy with an unusually wide stance named Ted Williams. And hidden in the shadows of the Yankee dugout, as yet unrecognized and awaiting his own destiny, sat a rookie named Mickey. Tempting as it is, I don't want to get too precious about this particular memory, because, to my mind, were it not for the grand spectacle of Yankee Stadium, these guys were no more exciting than my beloved GI teams back in Germany. I was getting homesick. By the time we flew back home a few weeks later, the Mannheim Little League was already holding tryouts for the new season and I couldn't wait to try out for a spot on one of the teams.

One of the teams picked me as a pitcher and shortstop. I had a good arm, but I was too small to throw a decent fastball, so my coach taught me how to throw a variety of wide, sweeping, curve balls that scared most batters and became my bread and butter pitch for years. Until puberty. After that, I started running into guys who were able to demystify the physics of my curve ball and send it singing *Hallelujah!* into the German mist.

In those days, there were no such things as weeks, months, or years. Only the next scheduled Little League game. On that day, the first thing you did in the morning, before blessing your marbles and baseball glove, was stick your head out the window and look for telltale signs of rain. Cloudy, gray skies were okay as long as they were thin and high, and not low and heavy. Doppler radar should be as accurate as a boy dying to pitch in a playoff game. That year we won the championship.

You'd never have been able to explain it to me at the time, but it was the spectacle of baseball that lured me into its field of influence, the science of the game that sucked me into its perimeter, the art of it that kept it interesting. What better way for a child to experience the physics of projectiles, velocity and distance, the geometry of bounces, obstruction by air and grass and red clay, the tractionology of cleats and stealing bases, climatology and games called on account of it.

After that, my memory gets progressively more foggy, probably because with each passing year my mind became more and more cluttered with abstract thought as I tried to cope with past and future, new concepts that evolved as the Prodigal Express traveled further and further away from Paradise Station.

I stuck it out as an altar boy right up through the eighth grade. It was then that I noticed there were almost no high school boys among the ranks of altar boys. When my own puberty arrived unceremoniously one morning, the urge to sainthood began to dissipate in the undertow of the gentle, irresistible sway of newly blossoming teenage girls. Not that I lost faith in religion, not then. I just selected a different role model, one Saint Augustine, who lived the life of an undisciplined hedonist for forty-odd years, then switched into saint mode. I adopted his time line as my own.

After baseball, came girls and wobbly rules. Baseball became a means by which inarticulate teenage boys, such as myself, could send out emerging masculine power signals to those sweetly developing feminine creatures who gathered in tiny groups on our periphery, waiting to try out their own growing powers of conquest. It's curious how, ever since Adam and Eve were tempted into taking a bite out of the knowledge of good and evil, that the loss of innocence has been tied to the breaking of rules. When I trace the loss of innocence in my own life, I must admit it's because someone broke the rules we live by, rules we believe are designed to keep our world safe.

Can you imagine trying to play baseball without rules, or rules that create less than the famous 'level playing field'? All things being equal, let's say one team is allowed to have twelve players on the field at one time and the other only six. Or, hits only count for your team if they go to the left of the pitcher's mound while the other team is allowed to hit anywhere in the field without foul lines. No one would accept such rules (some have no choice). Yet, what then of Babe Ruth's home run record which was set with softer, heavier balls, being broken by men clearly pumped up on illegal steroids hitting lighter, harder balls? Or the rule of loyalty? Mickey Mantle, Yogi Berra, and Whitey Ford all played out their careers with the Yankees. Ted Williams with the Red Sox, Willie Mays with the Giants. The Dodgers in Brooklyn.

One of my best friends, a Brooklyn Dodger fan, remembers the day the Dodgers moved to Los Angeles. He says that ended his childhood, so deep was the betrayal. With adolescence came rules of attraction and romance, many showing up in songs, such as "When I Fall In Love (It Will Be Forever)." Its harmonies infused the meaning deep into the teenage heart as "When Thou Fallst in Love, It Shalt be Forever." Can you remember the first time that rule was broken? The pain was searing. The second, third and fourth times, even more so. Listen to that song today or any of a thousand other songs and you find clues to the loss of innocence.

Innocence has an open heart. But the day comes, as it must, when we are betrayed. The heart is wounded. There are those who advise us not to even try to recall the first great betrayal in our lives. It is too great, they say; you don't dare remember it. It is far too painful. So to protect itself from ever again feeling such pain, the heart begins to harden and shrink, so as to be less of a target. The door begins to close. Then fear ascends, and speaks. "Listen for my voice," it says, "I will give you early warning. Together we will avoid those things that would hurt you." So you accept fear as a trusted ally, wrapping it around your heart to protect you, until the trusting voice of innocence is muted and the light of childhood grows darker and more discriminating. Only later do we find that fear itself is rooted in innocence and bravado. By then, however, the unspoken covenant with fear has all but strangled life of the risk and boldness that the eight-year-old keeps trying to remind us is still there.

So we go out into our world fully expecting that everyone understands that:

    1. The same rules exist for all
    2. They must be followed
    3. If they are broken, the offender shall be penalized.

and its corollary:

    4. If you don't want to get hurt, play by the rules.

These rules are always handed down from a higher source or from people we look up to. At first, our parents deliver the rules: don't play with fire; don't cross the street until after you stop, look, and listen; don't eat food that smells bad; put Band-Aids on a cut; be home before dark. They're health and safety rules, for the most part. Then religion steps in and issues its Commandments, powerful rules that seem immutable, but which are later found to have different interpretations, variations and origins. Perceptibly, rules change, shifting gradually in and out of focus. Thou shalt not kill, except in war and self-defense, or to punish those who have themselves broken that rule. Thou shalt not steal, except when following the rules of market capitalism, when greed is considered an acceptable, even admirable, Darwinian adaptation. But what about the those instances when the Darwinian "laws" of capitalism conflict with the natural "laws" of health? When that occurs, one rule might trump another, like, "Might maketh Right," which can cause enormous rifts between societies who play by different and sometimes opposing sets of rules. And, not everyone plays by the rule of "profit," which dominates our society and causes much of the world to look at us with something less than admiration.

So, looking back, the eight-year-old knew things I've long forgotten. He also knew that I would forget. Maybe that's why he sent messages to me in the future, messages of a heroic nature, having to do with destiny, meant to serve as guideposts to remind me of my source and destination. Instinctively, he knew I was teetering on the cusp of my own Fall from Grace, one foot planted in the Garden, the other about to step into the Dream of Separation. The messages were to be a lifeline, a reminder that the Garden is real. That said, half a century has come and gone and I'm still waiting. It's almost as if a letter written in one language was sent to someone who no longer understands it. Or worse, the message was scribbled down in the throes of a life-shattering LSD revelation:

"It's in the vegetables."

Stanley Peter Steinberg Day, Military Discharge Photo in 1943

The Wild West

Bob Flournoy

Bob Flournoy, 1953

Texas was everything that I had expected it to be and for seven years it became our home. I loved the endless expanse of desert to roam in with my BB gun, shooting lizards (which can absolutely ruin a load of wash when one is left in a pair of jeans). And my mother loved the climate, the people, the Mexican food and her first real house. I spoke broken, but conversant Spanish by the time I was in the fifth grade as a result of pure association with my Mexican classmates and our daily classes on the subject. We recited the Pledge of Allegiance without the words "under God" because the official addition of those words in the mid 1950s did not hit the school system until a couple of years later (I still forget to say them, since I did not learn it that way).

Texans were truly southern, but with a dash of something extra that gave them an even fiercer pride than the folks back home had; they were also western, and their history was barely out of the bare-knuckled phase in the early 1950s. They thought they were something really special. And they were. They were Texans. Texas was so mysterious to my mom and dad's Alabama parents that we may as well have lived in Japan, for what their limited traveling had exposed them to. We were in unchartered territory, before cable television and affordable air travel shrunk the country and the world. They figured that if they came to Texas, they would be able to take a day trip to Hollywood and check out the movie stars and the Pacific Ocean.

So, they were easily coaxed into visiting, and my parents dearly loved showing them their new world; a world of tacos and castinets, rugged rocky mountains, soft desert nights, pastel houses, sombreros, Juarez with it's colorful bullfights and markets, and dogs that could fit in a teacup. We had two, and they always found a seat underneath mine at the dinner table, having learned that various morsels—mostly peas, broccoli, liver and cauliflower—would somehow get secretly flipped off the edge of the table and onto the floor in the immediate vicinity of my feet.

My dad was stationed at Ft. Bliss, involved in the Army's first generation of guided air defense missiles; Nike Ajax and Hercules, as well as ground-to-ground missile development; Honest Johns, they were called. It was also the dawning age of jets and we lived smack in the middle of it. Those clear dry desert skies offered a perfect test scenario with Biggs Air Force Base just down the highway from our home, and White Sands Proving Ground was right over the Franklin Mountain range. In the six years that we lived in El Paso, we witnessed several generations of jet aircraft come and go as the Air Force experimented and tried to "get it right."

The air above us was filled with sonic booms and, all too frequently, black plumes of smoke that announced another crash. A "Cutlass" jet impacted the football field of my sister's high school, several blocks from our house, as the pilot declined to eject over such a populated area and chose, instead, to drive it into that small open area and prevent loss of civilian life. A German V-2 rocket that was being studied and tested at White Sands went astray and impacted in the mountains just above the city and scaring hell out of everybody. Brand new B-36's, B-47's, B-57's, B-52's, F-89's and F-100s took off and landed hourly, it seemed, in those early years of initial cold war arming.

I did not know a boy who did not build plastic models of these planes by the dozen or have whole squadrons of them hanging by string from his bedroom ceiling. We painted them, decaled them and sometimes blew them up with firecrackers, looking for that extra dimension of reality in our play. I can still hear my mom's words as I disappeared into my room with another unassembled model in its box, reminding me to "follow the directions this time." It was very hard to get the wheels on right when you had skipped ahead and glued the fuselage together first thing, so that the new work of art would begin to take on a recognizable shape as soon as possible. It had not yet occurred to any kid in the country to sniff that airplane cement.

It must have been the summer of 1954, which Fourth of July sticks in my mind, as an earliest memory of that holiday. That was our first summer in Texas and I distinctly remember being in back of the housing units that we initially lived in, running back and forth across a little road into a vacant field, exhilarated by the noise and confusion of the fireworks we were lighting. We were allowed such freedom as kids then; using firecrackers, cherry bombs and "M-80s" that are highly illegal today. Other than the rule about never lighting one in your hand, we pretty much had the freedom to destroy every prairie dog tunnel in the area, and we shot Roman Candles that were, to my recollection as a six-year-old, just short of space launches by today's standards. The mind set then was the same one that allowed us to roam freely with BB guns at an early age and hunt with the real thing not too many years later. Hey, it was Texas.

My son had the same burning fascination for fireworks at that age, and I remember when he was 13, letting him hold his own sparkler with me hovering closely by. Times have certainly changed. Luckily, we now have the government to protect us from such reckless exhibitions as our own personal backyard fireworks. It has taken over

200 years for Jefferson's nightmare to come true. Gone are the days when boys lugging around suitcases full of colorfully wrapped gunpowder could leisurely blow up ant hills, snake holes and sometimes mailboxes just for the thrill of it. And, in those days, firecrackers had fuses that would burn under water.

Our happiest moments were when we found a pothole that had minnows or tadpoles in it that could be blown into the sky. Fireworks also inspired creativity back then. I have a vague memory of a neighborhood dog running down the street with a package of "Black Beauties" on a string tied to its tail. That was an extravagant use of our limited arsenal, but worth it if things went off as planned; the only harm being a scared dog that took a lot of coaxing to get back home. And, of course, there were the predictable attempts by every kid in the country to get a cherry bomb or M-80 as high into the air as possible, with either a sling shot, or a bottle rocket that the ordinance was taped to. If you could get it to go off over some other kids down the block, or in a tree full of birds or squirrels, well, then you had something.

There were always rumors of a really big firecracker "out there" that you had to go to Mexico or Arkansas to get; so powerful and illegal were they, but, they were really capable of doing the damage that we desired. They were called something like "Big Buster," or "Widow Maker"; some label that inspired awe in us and created an image of destruction in its very name. We lived in anticipation of someday getting our hands on a bag of those, and every spring, as the Fourth of July approached, some kid would hint that an uncle or cousin was going to send them some. Anticipation would run high, with us asking the braggart everyday if the package had arrived. I don't recall that ever happening, so we had to improvise by twisting the fuses of our biggest bangers together, hoping that they would explode at the same time. Boys and their fascination for things that explode; we never had a chance a short decade later.

Later, we laughed out loud together as grown men when it became a vogue thing for the exploding "therapy" community to teach that girls and boys were essentially the same, doomed to turn out differently only because they were raised that way. Hilarious. I suppose there are those still making a living off of well-intentioned new parents by spouting that nonsense and keeping them off balance. No telling how much better we and our ancestors would have turned out if parents had always known these newly discovered secrets of child psychology.

We had wonderful neighbors in El Paso in 1955 who turned up more often than not on our patio to laugh in those still dry nights and who watched each others' children like they were there own. It was the glorious '50s, when everyone prospered and Ozzie and Harriet blared from the TV sets that more and more people were now able to afford. We cheered for the St. Louis Cardinals and Texas Longhorns and wore orange T-shirts. We rode our bikes with playing cards clipped to the spokes, hunted lizards and snakes, trapped prairie dogs, played baseball every chance we got, and started eyeing girls in a different way.

Hazel Lewis was my blond-haired beautiful classmate and neighbor and she had a younger sister, Jackie, whose face I can still see looking out of her bedroom window. Jackie had polio. Shortly after moving to El Paso, we had lined up in school to receive the new shots that would end this vile pestilence that struck fear in the hearts of all parents during the summer, and we felt very cheated when the very next year the class behind us got to eat their doses on a sugar cube.

Jackie was probably one of the last cases that struck American youth in that decade, and it had left her very sick. She had trouble breathing, and her family had moved to south Texas for the dry desert air that would supposedly give her a better chance. It was a hard thing for kids our age to digest, but we always knew that she was in there, in her house, in her bed. On the other hand, we thought nothing of living in houses that were hazy with the cigarette smoke of our parents. I remember the sterling silver and carved wooden boxes of cigarettes that virtually every home had on the buffet or living room coffee table, courtesies for visitors and guests. Those fancy boxes sure made what was inside them appealing: my first encounter with one of the three P's of marketing.

First Hunt

Bob Flournoy

Never living in one place for very long, my parents knew that we needed family roots and a sense of home that was more permanent than our transient lifestyle afforded. So in the days before interstate highways and air conditioned automobiles, we loaded up the family car every summer and drove to Alabama and my grandparents' farm. We usually made that two-thousand-mile round-trip across Texas and back in the summer, always gloriously welcomed by grandparents, aunts, uncles and cousins. Those visits are very happy memories.

I once reminisced with my mother about one of those trips when both of my dad's brothers, their wives and about six cousins were also present for a week in that little farmhouse. She gave me a raised eyebrow when I waxed sentimentally about the beauty of that time, but I remember it vividly. I was ten years old that trip, and something wonderful had happened.

Hunting, fishing and my anticipation of eventually making it to the big leagues pretty much occupied my thoughts at that age, but our time on that farm afforded me boundless fields, woods and swamps in which to hike and hunt with my dad and uncles. It was a glorious freedom and comradrie, the taste of which is still strong within me. Hunting and fishing were a way of life in this country in 1957, especially in the rural south, and I loved it. I was wild and free in the fields of south Alabama. But we had rules.

The rules were simple, and inviolate. Everybody knew them and obeyed them. Hunting and fishing on Sunday was unheard of, and no game bird was ever, *ever* shot unless it was on the wing. No ducks on the pond, no doves on the limb and no quail on the ground. You just didn't do it, and I never questioned it, although it made for some pretty long Sunday afternoons.

On this fateful trip, an unexpected surprise and trust was bestowed upon me, as one day I found myself alone with my grandparents. The rest of the gang had "gone to town." After bugging my grandfather to walk me through the woods with the old single shot shotgun that had been his as a boy, he told me to get the gun and a shell and follow him.

"One shell?" I asked.

"Yep," was his reply.

I hurriedly grabbed them both and followed my grandfather's arthritic limp across the cotton field that he had worked as a boy in the back of the old house and into the woods about 100 yards away. Thinking back, that walk must have seemed like a mile to him. When we finally stopped at an old wild pear tree, that could have been there since the civil war, my grand dad sat me down with my back against it and explained that if I was real still and quiet, a rabbit might come out of the underbrush for a fallen pear, and I could get it. He sat me down and slowly walked down the little dirt path back toward the house. I was stunned.

Alone? In the quiet woods with a shotgun in my lap. It just did not get any better. The quiet was a crescendo of whispering leaves and glinting sunlight, blending that golden space and time into an ecstatic rush of expectation. It was beautiful. I drifted, dreamed and imagined Creek warriors just behind the wild blackberry bushes. A perfectly racked stag was surely strutting toward me somewhere in the distant forest. Were those elves and sprites dancing about on the ground in the leaves just down the path that I was facing?

In a flash of regained consciousness, after I had been there for I don't know how long, my heart went cold and my hands clammy as it dawned on me what I was seeing. A male bobwhite quail had strutted out of the underbrush about 30 yards down the path and was bobbing his head up and down as he walked slowly away from me. Getting a rabbit had been a possibility in my mind, but a prized quail? Never. The dilemma was upon me. There it was, right there…on the ground. Aware of "the rules" and despairing over this disappearing opportunity as it meandered away from me, my mouth went totally dry when seven or eight more birds came out of the weeds and got in a perfect line behind their leader and strung out down the path. I couldn't stand it. No way. I raised the shotgun, elevated it to spread the shot evenly down the trail and pulled the trigger on that old scatter blaster.

In a roaring bang of smoke, the scene in front of me turned into a haze of dirt, twigs, dust, and…feathers. Lots of feathers. I was paralyzed. I sat there for a good five minutes before I raised myself up on shaking legs and cautiously moved toward the scene of the crime. A crime scene is exactly what it had become as I began to panic over what I had done. When I saw those fat, quivering quail lying in the path, my first instinct was to throw them in the underbrush and just go home, claiming to have missed a skinny little rabbit. No. Just could not do it. So, I picked them up, and, with their feet between my fingers I began the trek out of the woods and across the old cotton field to the back porch of the farm house where my grandparents, having heard the shot, were anxiously waiting for me, peering into the field for my appearance.

My grandmother, wringing her arthritic hands, started laughing with delight when she saw what I was carrying. My grand dad had a look of total consternation on his face like he could not believe his eyes. Not a word was spoken between us. Totally prepared to just 'fess up and take what was coming, I was not going to volunteer anything without his prompting. He took the birds and examined them silently. I trembled with resolve to just tell it like it was. My grandmother exclaimed with utter delight that she had never heard of three quail being taken with one shot! My grand dad brought his gaze up from the birds and looked at her. Then he looked at me and said, "Yessir, pretty fine shootin', 'specially as it appears these birds were flying upside down." And that was that.

We dressed those birds in the yard as the day dimmed and my grandmother cooked them for our dinner. I had never tasted anything so wonderful and still haven't to this day. The golden light that shimmered through the leaves of that old pear tree on that magical afternoon seemed to fill up the kitchen of that old farmhouse as I sat and ate those birds with my grandparents, 45 years ago. There is a snapshot of that scene in my mind now, as clear as the moment it was taken.

A Special Visit

Bob Flournoy

Christmas of 1955 was a big event for us, because my grandparents made the 2,000 mile bus trip from Alabama to be with us this time. Their slow, arduous trek across half the continent was made more wearying due to the absence of interstate highways and the necessity for that old Greyhound to stop in every little town along the way. But it was pure adventure to them. They loved it, and everyone on the bus loved them by the time they reached their destination. My grandfather spent days telling us everything that he had seen from a bus window, convinced that he had spotted things that were different than what we ourselves had observed, or at least understood them better.

He was fascinated by the whole experience, especially when we introduced him to Juarez and the love of bartering that the merchants there had. They met their match in him and he was convinced that no one ever had struck better deals than he was able to pull off, and he always left them smiling. He was finally left speechless after a day underground in Carlsbad Caverns and an evening sky turned black with bats emerging for a night of feeding. He would tell everyone he knew in Alabama about those bats. On the long car ride back home from that adventure, my mother turned around in the front seat and held a piece of fried chicken out to me, where my young sleepy head was resting in my grandmother's lap. I was not interested, but a snap shot of her smiling face holding that chicken breast out to me stuck in my mind. I was to hallucinate about it many years laterdeep in the jungles of Vietnam, having gone without food for three days.

I wanted a bike that Christmas. It was red, of course: one of those new skinny racing-type bikes that were beginning to replace the big fat tired clunkers. It was a Schwinn, a brand name which was synonymous with Cadillac as far as we boys were concerned. It was a stretch, but I wanted it. I asked my grandmother what she thought my chances were, and she advised strong sincere prayer on a daily basis. I got right to it. Several times a day. And little Jackie died. It destroyed the neighborhood and wracked everyone with a terrible sadness and grief that I can still feel. But kids move on, and on Christmas morning I woke up to a beautiful red Schwinn parked by the tree.

I rode it for miles and hours that day with a pack of boys who had also gotten new bikes. We rode with a wild hilarity and abandon that only young children can know, and I fell into my mom's lap that night after dinner, exhausted. After crawling into bed that night, my parents came into my room to tell me good night. Still believing in Santa, I asked my dad if he thought all of my praying had been responsible for the delivery of my new bike.

Ever the teacher, he looked at me for a long time, and said softly that praying was a matter of the heart. I was not sure what he meant by that, but I could not help but wonder whether or not Jackie's family had prayed for her life as hard as I had prayed for my bicycle, and why my prayer had been heard and theirs had not. Life moves quickly on for a child, however, and it propelled me and my friends onward toward fates that none of us could have foreseen when we were eleven years old.

Good Girls Follow the Rules

Sharon Fellows Larrison

Growing up a "military brat," learning to pack before learning to walk; moving, moving, and moving again. Always wondering, *Will I be the smartest in this new school or will I be the dumbest?* Fashion queen in one school often translated into laughter in another. The phrase, "It takes a village to raise a child," coined in today's world, was very much the case for military brats in the world of yesterday. While our fathers marched to military orders and to military bands, their children marched to the structured, often strict, households run by those used to giving orders. One step out of line and the *village* was on you and on your father. Adherence to the rules, spoken and unspoken, was the norm.

It was an innocent time for adolescents growing up in the late 50s and early 60s. Girls, too, loved baseball. We hardly knew the names of those big league teams or the big league players the boys bantered about. We could, however, recognize any one of our youthful ball player friends from a thousand yards, without ever seeing his face. The visual of a young man in a baseball uniform stretched tight across his buttocks was probably more titillating for the teen girls than a young man finding a copy of National Geographic with naked women from foreign lands. Sex was defined as male or female, an X in a box and nothing more.

Tradition, honor, and duty were the credo. Girls grew up, went away to college with no expectation except to find a mate, marry, have 2.5 children and live happily ever after. It was acceptable to work as a teacher, a nurse, or a secretary, and more acceptable to work only until the children were born. We grew up believing in our support role, focused on the betterment of our spouse. Our success was measured on our skills of homemaking, entertaining *his* boss, showing off the perfectly kept home and the perfectly kept 2.5 children. If we excelled at these tasks, our husband's career would advance, bringing us the rewards and happiness we expected. Cosmopolitan and traveled that we were, perfectly able to cope in foreign countries, with foreign customs, and always successfully overcoming having been the *new kid,* there was absolutely no glimmer of a life beyond those expectations set for us.

The Bronx
...and...
I could've been at that game

John Hopke

It was the spring of the year after the ecstatic October of the Dodgers' first World Series win. My love for baseball and, to their credit, my parents' support for my vital pastime, were both boundless. Without such passion, no tiny, skinny little-leaguer would have acceded to wearing his mother's garter belt under his heavy woolen uniform knickers in a last-ditch attempt to hold up his green stirrup stockings without resorting to a dangerous rubber-band tourniquet. How the white "sanitaries," layered in turn beneath the stirrups, maintained their elevation, I don't recall. It remains just as much a mystery as the sudden, and strangely almost imperceptible, elevation phenomenon that came ten years later, and may, come to think of it, also have involved a garter belt. (That was still a fairly common article of attire in the mid-'60s, but not, this time, on me, though slender I surely remained.)

In that rookie year of 1956, my father, a sergeant first-class in the Army Quartermaster Corps, attended one of the most famous baseball games ever played. He was stationed at a reserve center in the Bronx, base of the reviled American league rivals of my hometown heroes, and he permitted a security attendant at Fordham University, which was located near the Army facility, to park his car each day in the center's lot. The attendant rewarded my father in October with a pair of World Series tickets, so Dad took the afternoon off to attend.

I was quite accustomed to waiting on the enclosed porch of the family house in northern New Jersey for my father's return from work each day. I wanted the folded copy of the Daily News or Journal-American that always accompanied him; the ensuing evening's family activities were not what spiked my anticipation. Dinner was always a tense, dour affair, at which my two younger brothers and I were expected to "eat, not talk." And the bedtime hour meant burying my head under a pillow and muttering nonsense mantras as interference to counteract the loud discord that vibrated the marriage bed and the tiny hall space between us, and then silently reverberated through the entire house the next morning.

I had taught myself to read years before by poring over box scores of Dodger games in those newspapers Dad brought home. I already knew about Don Larsen's amazing, unprecedented accomplishment, and, as my father walked in the door, I brazenly said to him, "You didn't take me." He knew I'd be there, and he knew I'd have heard the perfect game on the radio. His obviously prepared attempts to assuage my selfish disappointment by declaiming about the boredom of the experience—only two runs scored!—did not soften my attitude or make me love him for his concern; they made me think him insensitive to such a degree that I was dumbfounded. I was doubly insulted.

Two years later, the stirrups fit better, I hit .300 or so to add some balance to a tight defensive game, and I made the league all-star team at third base. Although I was still the smallest kid on the squad, we were a solid crew, made up of the sons of the second-generation Irish-, Italian-, Greek-, and German-American insurance salesmen, blue-collar workers, and small merchants who lived in the southern part of our town, which was fringed by the meadowlands and marsh that have long since been filled, paved, and built upon by office complexes and hotels that append a pretentious 'e' to the end of the words like "point" that make up their names. Our individual teams were sponsored through the season by a pharmacy, the Firemens' Benevolent Association, a couple of insurance agencies, maybe a funeral parlor, some patriotic group like the VFW; all organizations with a feel for and a base in the sub-community, organizations whom we appreciated, patronized, and viewed as authority figures and models for our own futures, and whom we thought we might be able to reward with a bit of regional or national attention in the annual Little League tournament.

We never got to try. We had broken Little League, Inc. regulations by engaging in inter-league play. A team in my league called the Southern had beaten a squad from one of the other two leagues in town, causing the cross-town nine to lose its league championship; a disgruntled parent of one of the losing teams' players, in an act of spite, directed against our promising club, but which ultimately victimized her own kid, ratted to Williamsport. We were banned from the 1958 World Series, a series in which I would not have been able to participate, in any case, since my family was only days away from a departure to Germany, where we would join my father for the next two and a half years.

The Southern League All-Stars would have a degree of satisfaction, though, with or without me. A township championship series was arranged, and it proved to hold some significance for the residents of this growing suburb, for there were definable demographic and socioeconomic differences evolving between the various parts of town (although it wasn't until the next year when, as an infielder with an army-base Babe Ruth League team in Germany, that I played with or against black men), and the baby-boom generation, now ducking under desks in classroom air-raid drills and sliding under tags on dusty diamonds, would soon determine to an important degree everything from school curricula to zoning to property values in Hometown, USA.

One league was quickly eliminated from the tournament, leaving my group and the team from the league that perpetrated the Series ban. At this point, departure to Germany was two days away, my father had flown back to the states to escort us, and the family was staying with his sister in—-where else?—-Brooklyn. My parents drove me to New Jersey, a considerable *schlep* back then, in a car borrowed from another relative so that I could play in the final.

The weekday evening game went the regulation six innings without either team scoring, then three more the same way. In the top of the tenth, my team finally pushed a run across. And then the umpires called play to a halt on account of darkness, despite the high suspense everyone felt, and despite the awareness of my situation, which was graciously taken into consideration. It was just too unsafe and unfair to go on. With only one day left to prepare for an intercontinental move, my parents unhesitatingly decided to make yet another round trip from Brooklyn so that I could play what might only be three more outs. The next evening, we won the championship in that remaining half-inning, and I made one of the put-outs on a foul pop in short left.

I've thought often about my parents' sacrifices that evening and on other occasions, and I think their attitudes and actions toward us puzzled me and my brothers by contrasting so starkly to their actions toward each other. Why, I'd wondered even as a six-year-old, had the four of us not accompanied my father on his previous three-year Germany assignment? A young wife without her husband for so long? Three toddler and pre-adolescent boys unnecessarily permitted to grow up with out their father? I learned years later from my middle brother that my mother told him she'd been saving since the birth of the youngest for the day when she could leave my father, the man who once admitted to me he was acknowledged, probably even by himself, to be an "outside angel, inside bastard."

Our upbringing, in all respects, was extremely strict, formulated around Roman Catholic dogma and military guidelines. Directions, beliefs, practices, and causality were not reasoned out; they were simply accepted, memorized, and observed. And, of course, repeated verbatim when requested, as was the way with all public as well as parochial school educations in the 1950s. Learning was rote and unquestioned. (Indians and Mexicans were bad, and Davy Crockett—-interpreted, of course, as were so many of our legends and archetypes, by Disney—-was good.) Friends and allies were easy to recognize, and one spent much energy and money cultivating them, as did one's country. Building one's individual identity was sublimated.

Dad bought the drinks, told the jokes, was unctuously solicitous. Those of whom one disapproved were easy to know, too; of necessity, we associated, but did not socialize, with "Niggers," "Spics," and Jews. (I broke this taboo often, especially with kids with names like Silverman, Schwager, Sather, and Kahn.) On the broader scale, the great evil in the world were the Communists, who wanted to take away our baseball card collections, our *Mad* magazines, and our Blessed Virgin. (The last potential loss didn't much matter to me; *my* idol had become a 45 rpm dervish named Little Richard.)

There seemed to be a *quid pro quo* in the parental indulgence. There seemed to be a cultivated reverse dependency, something more than understandable parental pride, in and upon the academic, athletic, and social successes of myself (especially, as the first child) and my brothers. On that day each year that marked the birth of the afterlife's scorekeeper, December 25, we received a virtual roomful of gifts, a largesse, obscenely out of line with the family's meager means, which seemed to indicate, more than anything else, that we'd done well in the fifty-two preceding "innings." The tallies had been noted in report cards delivered, formulaic Saturday confessions rehearsed and delivered, runs delivered; and been found fitting, proper, and helpful toward salvation and the family's admiration by the community. Dad said so, the school authorities said so, Santa said so.

Back in Texas

Bob Flournoy

Bikes in a jumbled pile by the field; ignoring, in our haste to get out there and start playing, the commands of our parents to USE THE KICK-STAND!

We played baseball in those days from sun up until sunset. We played in empty lots, in the desert, anyplace that would accommodate a bunch of ten- and eleven-year-olds who went nowhere without their gloves, or mitts as we referred to them. It was, quite simply, a way of life for kids in the '50s. Our uniforms for organized games were merely T-shirts with a logo and color-matched hats, which we coveted more than money, and we prayed before games. We prayed to play to the best of our ability, and I remember one father coach praying for humility in victory. He always ended the prayer with "and, God, we *will* win this game. Amen." After all, there was a prayer before every major league game on TV, and didn't we idolize major league players and burn with a passion for the teams that we had chosen as ours?

It was easy to love a team in those days, because the players were seldom, if ever, traded. Our heroes were quiet and dignified and worthy of our admiration. They treated one another with respect and jogged around the infield after hitting a home run with their faces turned down, not wanting to embarrass the opposing team, especially the pitcher who had delivered the ball that was no more. The qualities that we worshipped in professional sports figures then are seldom, if ever, found in today's players. The Baseball Hall of Fame says that 95% of the rosters of major league baseball in the late 1940s were made up of veterans.

With a few exceptions, this era's what's-in-it-for-me guys do not inspire the kind of respect that we had for our idols, and curiously, I have not seen any hero-worship of sports figures in the life of my son or his friends, all of whom are avid athletes. It is as if they sense that today's players are uncaring, one way or the other, about what kids think of them. But the disappearance of those quiet teachers in the lives of boys has made it harder on fathers. Like neighbors who don't care as much as they used to, the village has grown smaller, the teachers fewer. But smiling graceful Willie, stoic Mickey, and dignified Ted had a place in our hearts, and we would not have disappointed them for the world.

I remember Alonzo Ramirez, one of the many great young Mexican kids I played with as a boy in El Paso. He always said he was half Apache and he might have been, because he looked at you with mean thirteen-year-old-eyes, towering above you on the pitcher's mound. It is true that pitching is partly the art of instilling fear in the batter, and I was scared shitless of him at eleven, but got lucky on him the next year. Some of those Little League pitchers could manage a big looping curve ball that frequently hit the dirt in front of home plate, but Alonzo had a side arm curve that snapped like a bull whip, to my eyes, just off your hip and zipped across the strike zone. One day, I flattened my bat out in back of me, parallel to the ground, and drug (too young and weak to yet be able to whip my wrists) it level to that side arm pitch, which broke flat. I became an instant celebrity by actually making contact with it, punching it down the first base line. From then on, his rhythm rhymed with my newfound batting posture and I had old Al's number. Yessireee…I had arrived.

After getting a hit off him my next time at bat, he blistered one at my head, hitting the brim of my hat, I was so concentrated on hitting the lower curve. Those things were okay back then, and a strong kid with good speed could own the plate and cover that short little league distance from mound to home with surprising suddenness. Wasn't there a famous pitcher years ago who had the nick name Sudden

Sam? Anyway, Alonzo's tactic worked until the sound of that bullet zipping past my face faded away and I was back on my newfound game, although for the rest of my baseball days, coaches, parents and players constantly tried to change my stance and the awkward way I held my bat. It may have looked funny, but it worked. Apache Al was a rightie, of course, and required a slugger brawler confrontation, as opposed to the rare leftie that came our way, with whom we danced and fenced.

"The Giants" 1957

A Different Kind of Grace

Bob Flournoy

Segregated in nineteenth century American schools from their right handed classmates, lefties were subjected to what can only be described now as an amusing discrimination by a society that demanded conformity on all issues. By God, they would not be allowed to use their left hands! It just wasn't *right*. As the game of baseball emerged and took shape in our culture, it is amazing that a leftie ever let himself be discovered as such on a ball field. But leave it to baseball to find those slight advantages in such a precise game that gave an edge to any kind of innovation whatsoever.

Imagine the elation of that first coach who discovered this talented genetic anomaly and realized the strategic edge that could be realized by fielding such a quirk. Home plates, originally located with a western orientation so that the lower passing of the sun throughout the day would not hamper play in our northern hemisphere, left a pitcher facing in that direction who could use his southern paw to keep an eye peeled on first base runners, and more fluidly whip a quick pick-off throw to keep his adversary honest. A hitter on that side of the plate, of course, had one less step to take en route to that first base, and the momentum of his swing would naturally put him in motion in that direction. Slight, almost imperceptible, split offensive and defensive seconds that are, in the long run, the difference between victory and defeat, where half a step is all that stands between a so-so hitter and a super star.

On a different note, I find myself at a loss, trying to verbalize in prose or poem the fluid movement differences that separate lefties from righties on the ball field. The graceful swing of a left handed pull-hitter, or the unimitateable overhand release of a southpaw pitcher, to say nothing of a Koufax curve ball. If you played the game, then you know. You can see it. It is discernable, yet unidentifiable. Like, poetry, or art, you know? I know what moves me.

You'll Never Go Far if You're Not an Eagle Scout

Bob Flournoy, III

And of course there was that first summer that the Boy Scouts opened their national campsite, Philmont Scout Ranch, in New Mexico, and my troop was privileged enough to be a part of the first Jamboree. I believe that was 1957 or 1958. It was bare bones then, with none of the facilities that it currently has, and we ran around like a band of wild Indians in those beautiful mountains, us being less supervised than some of the other troops that had formations and did projects and learned knots and stuff like that, which were all total distractions to fishing and climbing rocks and just generally goofing off.

On one of those days, a bunch of us from various troops were recruited to fetch dead fall wood from the surrounding forests, and the bigger boys spent hours pyramiding it into an enormous stack of wood for what would be a bonfire that night for a mysterious initiation right called the "Order of the Arrow." None of us knew what it was, but we knew it was going to be serious business. When the pile of wood reached about ten feet high and was complete and ready for the evening's festivities, a boy about my age named Steve Hook swore me to secrecy as he hid a one gallon can of vacuum packed pork and beans amidst the kindling, way back under the body of the wood that would soon be lit. I had no idea in my young mind what he was doing, and soon forgot about being a witness to the initial stages of the sacrilegious ambush that was going to occur far more successfully than old Steve ever envisioned.

Late that night, about 200 of us young bare-chested braves, dressed in loin cloths, found ourselves seated in a large ten-deep circle around that stack of wood, mesmerized as a dozen older scouts came out similarly clad, but with war bonnets and paint adorning their bodies. They slowly began to dance around the wood to the beat of a tom-tom drum, as one of them solemnly lit the kindling underneath. The pace of the drum picked up, as did the steps of the dancers, and it was all pretty dramatic to a bunch of eleven- and twelve-year-olds, I can assure you. Then, they started picking pre-selected boys out of the ring of onlookers by tapping them on the head with an arrow. When they were tapped, the initiates solemnly stood up and took their places in a ring around the fire, facing us.

As the bonfire roared and the tom-toms boomed and the painted warriors danced, a primeval rush of adrenaline flowed through the bodies of the younger boys. We would have taken up sticks or whatever and gone howling off to war right then, so caught up in the ceremony were we. When the fire exploded as a result of that vacuum packed can of beans not being able to expand anymore, a scene from Dante unfolded before our eyes.

All of the "tapped" boys and most of the dancing Indians were doing an entirely new kind of dance as they twirled and slapped and howled, trying to scrape the hot beans off of their backs and legs, not having any idea what had just happened. The kid next to me was wailing for his mom, as he had taken an unfortunate splash of steaming bean sauce right in the chest. Looking down at the sizzling mess, he kept screaming that he had been shot. There was utter and complete chaos as embers and sparks blasted skyward into the dark. Scoutmasters ran around without direction, shouting and cursing. Burning pieces of wood floated down from the sky, and 200 kids fled in every direction with hot beans in their hair and on their bare skin. Horrified, I knew that there was going to be hell to pay once order was restored, and I knew that I was in deep dookie as a potential accomplice.

Well, it took the better part of an hour to treat the wounded and put out the various other small fires that had sprung up in the surrounding brush and woods, and I think two tents burned from falling embers. You could feel the anger and outrage in the various scoutmasters as they got all of the boys lined up in formation in the wee hours after midnight and demanded that the guilty bombers identify themselves. Other than an occasional sob and threat of death and sexual dismemberment drifting out of the crowd, we were sober and quiet as one of the ranking scout masters went on an absolute spit-drooling tirade in front of us. We were told that we would stand at attention all night long until someone confessed. I was rigid with fear, almost catatonic, but faintly aware of a bad odor coming from the boy in front of me in the dark. I am pretty sure it was Steve Hook.

Well, after an hour, someone talked some sense into the cadre that had us locked and braced, and we were told to go to our tents with the certainty that someone would lose their head or be stoned to death at first light. We faded back to our sleeping bags in the dark, but it wasn't long before giggles and phrases like "real balls" started drifting out over the campground. We spent a wakeful restless remainder of the night, exhausted, yet intent on what the morning would bring.

Despite a morning of continued threats and general harassment, there was never a confession, and I never saw Steve Hook again after that camp-out. I think his dad was transferred or something, but he got away clean and I never squealed. However, later in the year on another camp-out, I caught my scoutmaster giving me a funny look when he observed me smirking at the sight of bean stains on his canvas tent.

A Real Military Brat

Bob Flournoy

We moved to Germany in the fall of 1959. I was barely 13 years old and not worried about the Cold War. I was worried about the availability of organized sports. I need not have fretted, because even in the midst of all that tension, the military always took care of its own, and that included paying special attention to the dependent children of the soldiers and airmen who were on call 24 hours a day. We lived in special housing areas that became small towns for us and each of these sported teams just like in "the world," with Little League and Babe Ruth baseball organizations.

I was eligible to make the big leap into teenage ball, but the obstacle of making a team seemed enormous, weighing heavily on my mind as the spring of 1960 approached. I had heard the rumors of how dominant some of the returning players were, able to hit home plate with a throw from centerfield, sliding with spikes high, etc., and it had not dawned on me that they were just kids like me. I had a fruitful and satisfying three years playing for the Pattonville Knights, traveling frequently to mystical places like Munich, Nuremberg, Frankfurt and Kaiserslautern. We also went to Berlin on blacked out troop trains through East Germany, to play against the boys in that isolated garrison, and we were there as the Berlin Wall was being built. We were warned not to open the blinds on the train because those East German guards, *vopos* they were called, would shoot with nary a qualm.

Our second baseman, John Miere, was elected to moon the German guards with machine guns in the black of night as we passed through some little village, because he was black himself. He was all for it and dropped trou as we rocked through the bahnhof of a small East German town and pressed himself against the train window while one of us opened the curtain. About the time that he chose to flash that young American smile into the heart of evil, John's backside was illuminated by the platform lights of that little station. With his camouflage protecting our insubordination, we sailed on through the danger zone, certain that, had one of us lighter skinned team members attempted that salute, we would all be dead. John, of course, became the subject of our praise as we retold the story over and over, and I am certain that this incident is part of the folklore of his family.

We were in Karlsrhue when the Cuban missile incident threatened to engulf the planet in nuclear war (civilians don't know how close we came), and I remember watching trucks full of troops, tanks, artillery and various other armored vehicles clogging the autobahns for miles as they all rushed to the Czech and East German borders. My dad was gone for weeks and we were packed and ready to evacuate back to the states on a moment's notice. Looking back, we would have had no time to do this. This became startlingly obvious to me not a decade later when I was a young officer stationed in Germany with a nuclear-capable field artillery unit. Eight years earlier, only 100 miles away, I had been preoccupied with sports and girls, oblivious to the ominous cloud that had hung over the world, and I now found myself with a top-secret clearance, responsible for the surety of eighteen nuclear warheads that guys my age were prepared to shoot at the bad guys if they chose to come our way. Unbelievable, looking back, but completely normal under the circumstances.

One of the proudest moments in my young life was when my commanding officer, a man I greatly admired and respected, put his career in my hands by giving me charge of the battallion's nuclear weapons section. There was no room for even a hint of an error in that area, and more than one career was ruined by not paying attention to the minutest details. It is truly amazing that no branch of our armed forces ever had an accident or a noteworthy incident involving nukes in the many years of the cold war when those weapons were deployed and on station. At its core, the military never lost its sense of duty and professionalism, even in the challenging years of the '60s and '70s, when Vietnam pressures so severely challenged morale.

We got to proudly wear our game jerseys for whatever sport we were playing in junior high school, so a couple of us had our baseball jerseys on one day in the spring of eighth grade, standing out from the crowd and feeling cocky. At lunch we sat side by side at long folding tables, on metal folding chairs, a pretty standard arrangement, which is probably what you would see in a school lunchroom even today. Girls wore dresses to school back then, and Becky Watson, snooty little thing that she was, always wore the frilliest. She was so aware of herself in those lacey things that she would compliment herself constantly and inevitably became the object of 14-year-old boys' taunts and snide remarks. Nasty, but normal.

On this particular day she was sitting across from me at lunch, all prim and proper, jabbering away, when Lee Lasiter got up from the seat down the table and, with a mischievous glint in his eye, walked behind her and held up a pat of butter for all to see. About the time that Becky saw all of us at the table in front of her go wide-eyed with anticipation as we stared over her head, Lee dropped the butter down the back of her dress before she could spin around to see what was going on. As the sensation of slime hit her skin, one of my friends next to me cried out, "No, Lee, not a frog!" and about that time old Lee slapped Becky's back where the butter had come to a sticky rest, and of course it went "kersplat" and Becky, with the image of frog guts fouling her dress and bare back, let loose with a technicolor upchuck of ketchup, wieners and relish that her subconscious must have envisioned as an exorcism of the mess on her backside.

This stunning display of self defense set off a chain reaction in the other girls and boys who were sitting in the vicinity, the result of which was a work of mesmerizing abstract on the table which slowly oozed and spread onto the laps of the stunned onlookers. It was a real nasty mess, Becky wailing, boys laughing and girls gagging, and when the bedlam subsided, poor old Lee got suspended for three days. From my perspective, it was worth it, although I feel a little ashamed after all these years at how poor Becky must have felt. If any boy had ever done that to my daughter…

An Extraordinary Lesson

Bob Flournoy, III

My freshman year in that American high school in Germany provided me with a rare teacher who left a lasting impression on me with his caring and dedication to his profession. He was our physical education teacher and he was British. Probably about 40 years old at the time, he had grown up in England in the years leading up to and then during WWII. A man whose male ancestry had been virtually eliminated in the first world war, along with the better part of his father's entire generation, he was teaching in the American school system on the continent, for what reason I do not know. But one day he told us a memorable story of how, as an exchange student in 1936, he and some fellow high school students had traveled to Berlin as guests of the new Nazi government, so that the two cultures could cement their mutual regard for one another and show off a little bit. War between Germany and England was still several years away, and Hitler's dream of showcasing the master race was coming true that year in Berlin, where the Olympics would be held.

One night, around 1 a.m., when my teacher and all of his 16-year-old friends were asleep in the barracks that they had been quartered in, they were awakened with bright lights and much ado, and hustled out the door onto waiting buses. The night was pitch black, with no moon or stars, and the route that they were taken on to their mysterious destination was also carefully blacked out. They had no idea where they were going and, when they arrived, they could see nothing of their surroundings.

Cordially, but efficiently, their German hosts lined them up in what appeared to be a parking lot, and marched them silently through what felt like a tunnel, or between some large structures. Eventually they were stopped on what felt like a field of grass and ordered to be very still. The quiet was deafening, with not a breeze stirring, nary a cough or whisper evident on the dead calm night air. Then, in a soft voice, when the silence had become crushing, one of their Nazi hosts spoke to them, and told them that physical education was not only about disciplining the body, but the mind as well, and that he would like to demonstrate what he was talking about.

With that, he snapped his fingers and the English students were blinded by a thousand powerful lights that revealed to them, after the shock of their brightness wore off, that they were standing in the middle of the new Olympic Stadium. The stands were shoulder to shoulder with 100,000 young German school children, dead silent, mute, and staring down at them.

A Real Coach, A Real Man

Bob Flournoy, III

The summer after my freshman year in high school was my most memorable season in baseball. We beat everyone and I hit everything that came across the plate. We had a wonderful man for a coach who donated his sparse spare time to us. The military of that era, as it is today, was a very multiracial society. I went to school and played ball with blacks, Mexicans, Phillipinos, Guamanians, Japanese, and many more skin colors than I can remember. We thought nothing of it and, oblivious to what society's prejudices might have been, we were all just kids in school, dancing at the youth center or on the ball field.

Our coach, Sergeant Cole, was black and had the sweet disposition that was necessary to keep a bunch of 15-year-old hooligans corralled and focused. One day, being a bunch of smart-asses, we started teasing him by calling him Amos and Sambo. It was harmless stuff to us and reflected our affection and comfort with him. He quietly ordered the practice stopped and brought us all in to the pitcher's mound, where he had been throwing batting practice.

In a measured, patient voice, he said to us, "My name is not Amos. My name is not Sambo. My name is Sgt. Cole, and I am out here with you on Saturdays and after work so that you have a team and someone who cares about you. I also am a platoon sergeant for an armored cavalry regiment that will surely be the first to die if the balloon ever goes up. I spend many days and nights in the field, away from my family, but I never miss a practice or game or time for you when I am not out there. Are there any questions?"

You could have heard a pin drop, such was our shame, as we quietly returned to our places on the field. I would give anything to find that man today.

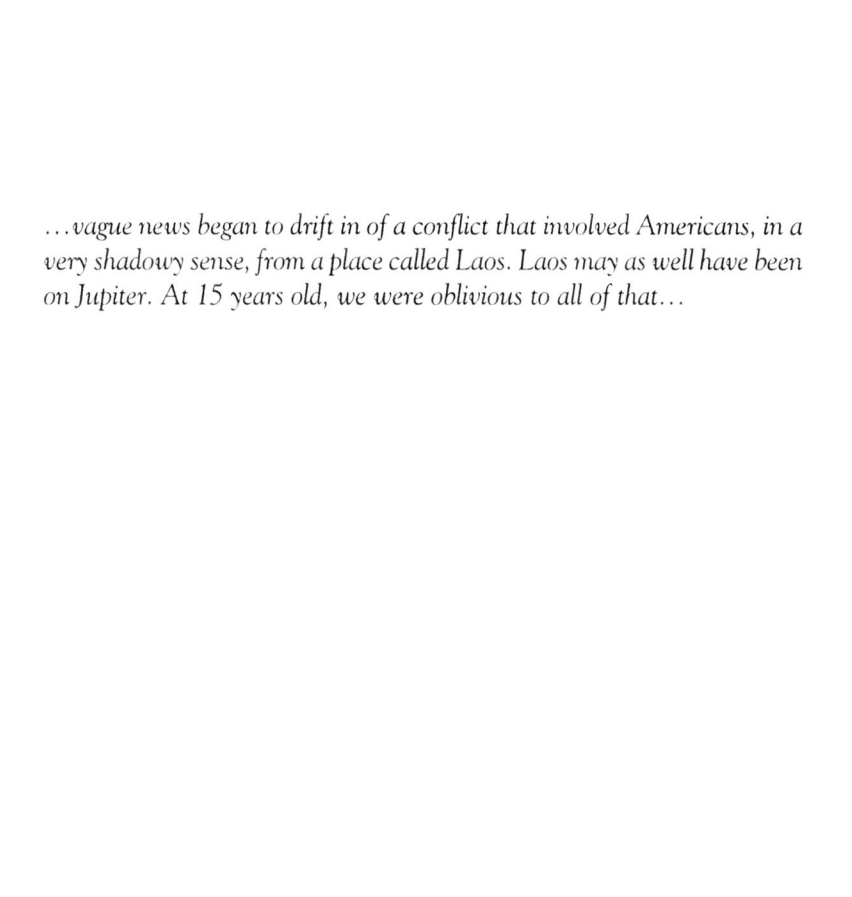

…vague news began to drift in of a conflict that involved Americans, in a very shadowy sense, from a place called Laos. Laos may as well have been on Jupiter. At 15 years old, we were oblivious to all of that…

Birmingham, Alabama, 1920s

Bob Flournoy, Jr.

There were 22 preteen children on the one block where I grew up. Everyone knew every name and to whom each belonged, which was incidental because all the grownups were in on the raisin'. There were at least half-a-dozen front doors that I could traverse as readily as my own. There was a grand total of three moving vehicles on my street: the next door cop's motorcycle, a pickup truck that was a neighbor's drive-home from work, and a Pontiac four-door sedan belonging to a family of two working parents; the only one in my memory.

Mine was a new grammar school, and everybody lived within walking distance. It was a good thing, because there was no such thing as a school bus, and hardly anyone owned an automobile. Weather was no hindrance because we didn't know any different. I vividly remember every one of my teachers. They were all female and not allowed to be married; marriage was considered a distraction. The school was ultra-nice, well-equipped, and had a huge recreation area out back with a slide, swings and monkey bars for the girls. Our auditorium teacher, who doubled as the playground teacher, called on a genuine English neighbor to teach us to play soccer (a brand new game). There was also a tennis court, and our summer activities teacher taught us to play. She also taught me to play a harmonica with an instrument I bought with 10 octagon soap coupons. She was killed in an automobile accident, which was my first experience with death.

All play among my friends was improvised. There were distinct seasons for all games, unannounced, for we just knew when each time was right. There was baseball, marbles, roller skating, and that included "shinny," played like ice hockey with hickory limbs for sticks and a beat-up condensed milk can for a puck. As we grew a little older, we graduated to sand lot, full contact football, in which I broke my right arm. It was during the week of "achievement tests" and I took them all writing with my left hand. I was moved up to the next, fifth, grade ahead of my class the following semester.

Most of my summers revolved around at least some time spent with my grandparents and/or my aunt and cousins. All of them were alive and well and role models, each in their own way. The New York Yankees did their spring training in St. Petersburg, Florida, the home of my maternal grandparents, during the time of Babe Ruth. The Babe was a friend of my cousin's best friend's family, and on this big occasion when he was visiting the friend's home, I was introduced and got a handshake and a head tussle from the Babe himself. My daddy was a firefighter and could attend all kinds of things free, so when the Yankees later played an exhibition game with the Birmingham Barons, Dad took me down to the dugout, where Babe Ruth remembered me and I had a second handshake.

High school for me was a glorious adventure. I was a three-year starter on the football team and ran 220-yard anchor on our track team that set a new state record for the half-mile relay. Academics came easy, as did relations with my many friends. Mother and Dad attended all of my athletic events, and many of my friends developed fond relationships with them. There was no way I could look forward to college in the middle of the Depression, until a close family friend offered to pay for my room and board at Alabama Polytechnic Institute (later Auburn University) so I could "walk on" and try for a football scholarship.

I entered Auburn in the spring quarter, in time for spring football practice, went out with the team and earned a full scholarship. I attended Auburn for two years, during which I attained a private pilot's license in the government's special training program, designed to give prospective Aviation Cadets some flying experience. I dropped out of

Auburn with the intent of applying for the Cadet program, as did most of the men in my flight training class. I wanted flying to be my life. Upon entering the cadet program, I was selected to be an exchange student with Britain's Royal Air Force. Upon graduation I was commissioned in both the RAF and the USAF and was assigned to the USAF Air Transport Command with station in India to fly supplies across the Himalayas to China, dubbed "The Hump."

A firm belief that peeing on the tail wheel of my airplane got me safely through 102 missions. During this time, my brother Browning was a marine on Iwo Jima and my brother Dick was in the Army and headed for Italy. I tried not to think of them. There was nothing I could do. At the end of WW II, I returned to Auburn University to earn a degree in Electrical Engineering and, after a short time of employment with the TVA, was recalled to active duty for the Korean conflict. I flew as a General's Aide and personal pilot, while also taking my turn as an Artillery observer. My boss was a Corps Artillery Commander who flew over his firing batteries every day, and on this flight we saw an F4U Corsair Marine fighter plane wreckage on the bank of a small stream. We landed close by, to possibly be of assistance, and came upon a figure in flight gear kicking the remains of the wreckage and swearing hotly…maybe the world's greatest baseball hitter, Ted Williams.

I don't remember the Birmingham Barons being part of any major league baseball organization, but they provided the nuance for all preteen baseball in the city. In the middle of the Great Depression, there were many vacant lots that provided "home" fields in almost every neighborhood. Real baseball gloves, bats and balls were to dream about. In nearly every instance, bases were any soft material hammered into the ground, home plate was a lid of any sort, and the pitchers' box was a half-buried brick or two by four laid lengthwise.

Teams were the kids who lived on your block, and up-the-road frequently played down-the-road; or sides might be chosen from whomever might be present. "Little League" was a term being bandied about, but never reached my neighborhood; Babe Ruth ball was a promotion for teenagers sponsored by local businesses. The only coach I ever knew of was the superintendent of the Birmingham schools and father of a player on a team from the Catholic school. Their team was organized enough to invite us to play a game on our "home" field. When they arrived, they unloaded a 15-year-old fastball pitcher on us who knew every pitch in the inventory, and when the game was called after an interminable three innings, most of us had sworn off baseball for life. It didn't matter too much, because most of us had gone on to high school and taken up with football and track. No fast-ball pitchers there!

We also began each game with a ritual that we called Scrub-1 (don't ask me). Maybe the first one on the scene says to the group gathered there, "Scrub one." He who first yelled "scrub one" gets to toss a bat, knob end up, to another one of his choice. The catcher of the bat, small knob up, grips it where he caught it. The "scrub one" then grips the bat above and touching the catchers hand. The catcher then grips the bat above and touching the other's hand, and so forth until there isn't a hand's width left on the bat. If the last catcher can then grip the knob and toss the bat over his shoulder, he gets first pick from the pool for his team. If he can't, then the tosser gets first pick. Choices back and forth then until everybody gets picked. Play ball! Scrub-1…

The Game Has Changed

Mike King

In the mid '50s, baseball was truly the American past time and a game unique to this country. It was a time when baseball heroes would willingly leave the game and go to war to fight for their country. Ted Williams missed about 5 years during the prime of his career, fighting in two wars. He did this initially after hitting .406 in 1941. In the '50s, our heroes played baseball for the love of the game. They did get paid, but salaries were in line with what mere mortals made and they related to and came from meager common stock just like us. The players had respect for the game, each other and the American way. They gave their word and stuck to it. There was no renegotiating contracts in mid season and no arguments with other players, managers and owners through the press. The slider was coming into being as was the forkball, now called the split finger fastball or splitter. There were few specialty positions such as DH, or long or short relievers, or set up men. You could sit in the bleachers in left field in Yankee stadium for 75 cents even as late as 1969. There were characters that were as unique as the quirks of the game that brought color and life to the field. They were loved although some did not contribute to the financial bottom line. Batters crowding the plate could expect "chin music" and got it. Players played 9 innings a game for 154 games a year barring injury. Teams played team ball. The World Series was truly a special event and games were mostly played in daylight. There were quirky ball parks of which only a hand full remain including Wrigley Field and Fenway Park. Teams were not just representative of a city, but an entire region. The Red Sox are still an example. Fans would scream epithets at the opposing teams, but never throw stuff on the field or at other players.

Today's game is about big business and the individual. Megastars can demand that their contracts be renegotiated at any time. They can demand certain personnel be moved, such as managers, or other egos that they do not get along with. Mediocre pitchers can earn millions of dollars a year. Some are there only to face a few batters in any given game, just to set up the closer. Specialization is the name of the game. There are designated hitters that never have to become defensive liabilities to their teams. Players are juiced, that is to say enhanced by steroids. Drugs are rampant and players pretty much care about themselves first as there are billions of dollars being exchanged and they feel that their first responsibility is to themselves with fans being a distant second. Expansion has diluted the talent pool. Players today are better conditioned than the players of yesteryear and there is no off season. Baseball is now an international game and an Olympic sport.

Many of the major league players today are from the Dominican Republic, Cuba, Puerto Rico and other parts of central America. Increasingly, players are of Asian background and there are professional leagues in Japan and Latin America during the US Major league off season. Many players play year round. We have major league teams in Canada. Mexico is logically next. Individual stats are more important than team stats. You would never ask a Barry Bonds to lay down a sacrifice bunt in today's game. The baseball itself is juiced (wound tighter than in the past) and baseballs are flying out of cookie cutter ball parks with hitter friendly backgrounds and dimensions. Even the busts in Yankee Stadium, which used to be in play, are now behind a moved in fence in center field. Owners demand new ball parks financed by cities or they threaten to move their teams to places where they can get a better deal. It is about business and litigation. The sport has left the game. All this is sad, but change is inevitable, and it is still baseball, which I love.

War Comes Calling

Bob Flournoy, Jr.

Robert W. Flournoy, Jr., 1943

...In 1942 I was working in a munitions plant on a job that was classified as "essential to the war effort," and not subject to the draft. However, with a young daughter coming on, I was determined to have an appropriate answer when she might ask, "What did you do in the war?" and besides, I had yearned for some time to enlist in the Army Aviation Cadet program. In order to apply, I had to volunteer for the draft and obtain a release from the E.I. Dupont Company. When these matters were cleared, I applied, was tested and accepted and, after Pre-flight, was nominated as an exchange student to train with England's Royal Air Force.

Due to a shortfall of space and facilities, this was to take place in Miami, Oklahoma. I was an able student, and my wife and young daughter were on hand for graduation. During the graduation parade, my daughter caught sight of her daddy marching past, evaded her mother's grasp and ran toward him. As she passed by the reviewing stand, she was picked off her feet by the Commandant, and viewed the march-past from his uniformed shoulders.

After a short stint at an airbase in Great Falls, Montana, I was sent to an Army Air Corps base in Sookerating, India, to fly supplies over the Himalayan mountains to our ground forces in China. This operation became familiarly known as flying "The Hump." The routes required flying at extremely high altitude through, possibly, the worst weather in the world. There were distinct seasons of monsoon, with winds of three-digit force, and year-round conditions were totally unpredictable and usually rampant. On one flight, I reckoned it took a 170-mile-an-hour wind to take me so far off course, but that's another story. At age 23, I was aircraft commander of a C-46 type aircraft, flying the Hump from August 1944 till the war's end in August 1945. This involved 102 round trips to various bases in China, carrying supplies, and performing in a couple of special operations. Some of these involved flying Chinese coolies back to training bases in India, and even hauling mules to forces in Burma. The coolies were flown sans parachutes and warm flying gear, and under protest by the pilots.

My first mission was as co-pilot for an experienced veteran who was completing his "tour." With starting-gun jitters, I had an urge to pee. I performed this act at the rear of the aircraft, near the tail wheel, and this little ditty became a token of habit because I had lived through my first mission; which wasn't the case of a very good friend with whom I had traveled to India. That, too, is another story. My radio operator, a permanent part of my crew, was a great kid of 19. On this occasion, he approached "my" tailwheel and I shooed him off, saying this was for officers only. Not until later, after a particularly hairy mission, did he ask, "Now may I pee on your tail wheel?" He did, and proudly! Josh Gibbons volunteered to extend his tour of duty due to a shortage of radio operators in the theater, and asked if he could fly with me; the greatest compliment I could receive.

The Hump was first attempted with the C-47 "goony bird" type aircraft, a work-horse since the '30s. It, however, proved to not withstand the poundings from the weather over the mountains, and also had a limited payload capability. Thus, the C-46 Commando was introduced, and went into service without any operational testing. It was half-again as large as the '47, with twice the payload, powered by two Pratt & Whitney R-78 two-stage, supercharged engines producing 2,000 horsepower each. It had a beefed-up airframe that could take the weather, and with its hydraulic and electrical faults, it went into service. The first went to a transition school in Reno Nevada to check out a few instructor pilots who, in turn, checked out the replacement pilots arriving with the new aircraft in India. It was a learn-as-you-go operation for both personnel and equipment. The engines on the C-46 were ultimately upped to 2,200 horsepower and the payload increased from 48,000 to 52,000 pounds. The aircraft were delivered with hatches, heaters and windows, all of which were removed as part of the effort to maximize payload for delivery in China. At a common altitude of 30,000 feet, temperatures could reach 65 degrees below zero, making heavy leather flying gear essential. Conversely, there was no more breath-taking sight in the world on a rare clear day, with the likes of Mount Everest and other mountains of proportionate height in the background.

I was introduced to a memorable man on a return flight from China, when my number-one engine went out and I was forced to land at Shimbwiang, Burma. A C-47 aircraft had crashed into the jungle upon take-off and one Bill Devore, who was part of a search-and-rescue unit at Mohenbari, India, was summoned to do his thing; i.e. jump into the wreckage as he had done on over 100 other occasions, to assess, maybe treat, and possibly evacuate survivors.

He stepped out of a C-47 at 300 feet altitude in a pair of khaki shorts and combat boots, with a walkie-talkie radio and a .45 caliber pistol strapped to his hip. Upon landing at the sight, he radioed the situation to the group at the base: one dead and one with a broken back. He then outlined what he wanted dropped to him: so much dynamite, rope, block-and-tackle, etc,. so he could cut a runway out of the jungle for a small-plane landing strip. They did and he did, all through the night, until the next morning when sufficient space was cleared for an L-5 aircraft to get in and out.

A Captain Taylor, the officer with the broken back, was strapped to a hard litter and flown out in the small plane, surely saving his life. This was only one of several types of rescues by this amazingly resourceful man. The tales are many that could be told about things experienced "Flying the Hump." Many aircraft and flight crews were lost across an "aluminum highway," paved with those who went down.

After WWII ended, and staying on for another year, I took a four-year absence from active duty to complete degree requirements at Auburn University. Utilizing a degree in electrical engineering, I had taken a position with the TVA, where I was employed when North Korea invaded the South across the 38th geographical parallel. I quickly volunteered for recall to active service, but as an Army aviator in the Artillery. I had that choice, having served two years in the Army National Guard, while retaining my reserve status as a pilot in the newly created United States Air Force.

Upon reporting in to Fort Sill, Oklahoma, I was selected to fill an aviator's slot in the newly reconstituted VI Corps Artillery. This new headquarters was to be commanded by BG Thomas E. Lewis, who had been General Mark Clark's Artillery Commander during the Italian campaign in WWII. After a short refresher in both light airplane flying and Army Artillery, General Lewis asked me to accompany him while he served as Senior Army Representative on a newly organized Board to refine means of providing close air support by the Air Force for Army ground troops. General Lewis requested, and was assigned to, Korea, as Commander of Artillery in I Corps. He asked me, and I agreed, to accompany him as aide and personal pilot.

I Corps occupied the left flank of United forces on the Korean Peninsula with IX Corps in the middle and X Corps in the East. General Lewis looked over his Battalions and especially the firing Batteries daily, by air. This, combined with taking my regular turn on combat patrol, gave me a lot of flying time. A bond developed between General Lewis and me, which was threatened on a cold snowy night at Christmas time in 1951.

Gathered around the M-41 stove in the Operations tent, General Lewis said, "I want to fly to X Corps Artillery HQ."

I said, "No, sir, not tonight."

I thought I had said it in a light tone, but he said, "Are you refusing to fly me?"

I said, "Call it what you may, General. I couldn't find my ass with both hands in this kind of weather!"

And thus was born what became the General's trademark utterance of frustration, "Well, piss on the Pope."

He stalked out of the tent and we didn't fly that night. All was well the next morning when I flew him to Tageu to request the assignment of two individuals, with whom we both had served on the Air Support Board, Major Bill Edler to be his Air Officer and MSGT. John Kagan his HQ Btry First Sergeant. Both were assigned to him, which raised his spirits and mine.

On another night, with reports of incoming enemy fire, General Lewis said, "There must be a way to return fire."

This time I told him that there was a way, kinda' far out, but it could work. I bartered, from Air Force logistics, a transmitter crystal for the tach radio in my light plane so I could communicate with an Air Force guidance center that was using radar to guide their bombers on night bombing missions. With this facility I could have them lock onto me, stand by to "mark" my position, and direct them to mark when I placed myself over an Artillery flash on the ground. They, in turn, could send eight-place coordinates to our fire direction center, and we then could call down return fire. It worked, and worked so well that we continued air patrols through every night with very good results.

"JUST A LITTLE RAIN..."

I left General Lewis in Korea when he sent me home "To be with your family." I didn't see him again, but did try to call him on the phone once when passing through San Antonio. When I asked to speak with the general, Mrs. Lewis said, "Tom's at the golf club."

I laughed and told her that the general had always said there were two things he would not do on retirement: play golf and putter around the house. Then she laughed and said, "Bob, he isn't playing golf; he and his cronies are playing polo with the carts!"

...we lay anchored off shore for weeks and took comfort in the devastation that the Navy and Air Corps were delivering on the beaches and jungles of the island that awaited our assault. We knew that absolutely nothing could live through a pounding the likes of which we were witnessing. Confident that our occupation of Iwo Jima would be met with little resistance, I was stunned speechless at the expanse of dead bodies that littered the sand and surf when I first stepped onto that hell. None of the dead were Japanese...

George Browning Flournoy

The War Comes Home

Bob Flournoy

My senior year in high school, we frequently ate dinner on TV trays in the den, or we watched a portable television on a small table in the dining room (another small erosion in the landscape of the American family); the resulting was a loss of family talk time. We would watch reporters who were starting to report from the field in some place called Vietnam, mostly with advisors and green beret outfits. It was all very exotic at that point. A few months later, the first semester of my freshman year in college, the nation was shocked when units of the 1st Cavalry Division, which I would join years later, suffered 200 casualties in one battle, killing over 2,000 of the enemy in three days. Body counts were legitimate during this early stage of the war. As a result of this encounter, the enemy would learn to "hug" us, and the nature of the war would take an ominous turn. Friendly fire deaths would begin to rise as "close" artillery and air support would take on an ominous new meaning, with associated risks, and fatalities.

Casualties were running 300 to 500 Americans killed per week by 1968, with six times that number wounded. We were killing ten times that number of Viet Cong and NVA, so we supposed that we were winning. Our losses seeded a venomous mind set into the troops in the field, and the viciousness of the fighting increased, hatred flowing deep and steady on both sides. I watched in detached numbness, and, while away at school I read, in a dazed state my parents' letters which would too often refer to another high school classmate who had died. My high school lost 37 boys before it all ended. One high school. Two were close friends and only children. Gone, and now, all the parents, also gone. Families ended completely, forever, like they never were there; the echoes of their passing drowned out by the noise of different families sleeping under those same roofs.

Lance Corporal Bronson Westfall, my childhood friend and classmate, was killed in 1967 by a Marine Corps mortar round that fell short of its intended target to his front as his squad was pursuing enemy troops. When his body was returned to his hometown of Hampton, Virginia, several weeks after his death, his father, Manny, went to the local airport to receive his only child and identify his remains. The body that Manny viewed was headless, and a telling scar that Bronson had on his body could not be found. Manny, and his wife, Ginny, both now dead, spent the rest of their lives hoping.

Bob and Bronson, 1963

War Zone C, Republic of South Vietnam

Bob Flournoy, III

Bob Flournoy, December 1971

...We stayed out 22 days my first mission. After walking off of a tiny landing zone in a remote jungle, splitting up so as not to give away our ultimate direction of travel, the company linked up at a rendezvous point kilometers away. Hooking up in the deep bush was touchy, since this was the only time that you didn't shoot first and talk later when running into someone "out there." Friendly forces exchanged fire more times than we would like to admit on these occasions. When we slept, it was on the ground, as flat as possible, never taking off boots or covering up. We never talked, we whispered, and we used hand signals to communicate. A whole language of breaking squelch on the radio developed, negating the need for any verbal noise. We wore no underwear or socks in that fecund, hot, wet hell; they quickly stank and rotted, as we were always wet. Our skin fell off in soggy green pieces from jungle rot. Groins were especially susceptible to this condition and I remember men lying in the sun when possible with their trousers off, legs spread to its warmth and dry heat. Soldiers relieved themselves on the spot, feeling vulnerable to the darkness around them, never letting go of their weapons; a couple of images for those who would gender integrate the military to ponder.

Groups of 10 or 40 very young men, boys, moving silently through the jungle, single file, five meters apart, with 70 lbs on their backs for 10 hours a day. Young killers from Omaha, Montgomery, St. Louis and New York, on edge with atavistic instincts awakened from some primeval time, adherents to a ritual painfully learned and bequeathed by those that had walked before them. The war was eight years old at this point. Our families would not have believed it, and Hollywood has never come close, not once, to getting it right.

There is no combat footage and almost no still photography of the Vietnam War that accurately depicts how it was fought on the ground, in the jungles, at night, at point blank range in exchanges so violent, savage and quick that each encounter was often over in minutes, seconds even. Photographers were seldom allowed in these settings and, if they were, the events' ferocity prevented any kind of adequate recording. How do you film the mind-numbing, strobe-light-flash blast of a claymore that a trip wire sets off when it is least expected and the mad minute of small arms fire that ensues? The scenes that TV has shown of soldiers lined up, firing their weapons, or sitting behind a wall exchanging shots with an unseen enemy are either staged or in such low intensity contact that they don't come close to showing what soldiers were faced with.

"JUST A LITTLE RAIN..."

Always wary of the dark jungle around us, we were also very much aware of the 18 year olds behind us who had nervous fingers on the triggers of their chambered automatic rifles. Accidents and friendly fire accounted for at least one-third of the American deaths in Vietnam. Some would put that figure higher. Much higher. I was an artillery forward observer with an air cavalry infantry company in the First Cavalry. My RTO, born in 1954, was 17 years old…

Hot Was Just Fine With Me

Paul Cowan

Michigan was the state where I grew-up, and Muskegon was the town, right on Lake Michigan. The lake resembled the Gulf of Mexico, with its modest surf, sugar-white sand and big, high dunes. That similarity ended with the appearance of icebergs in the winter and water so bone-chillingly cold, even in August, that "Your lips are blue!" was a common comment heard after one had spent barely 10 minutes in the surf.

Muskegon in the 1950s was a pretty simple place. We played all day and half the night; kick-the-can, duck-on-a-rock, chase, war, king-of-the-hill, hide-and-seek, and anything that had to do with a ball. Depending on the weather, it was kickball, basketball, baseball, football or variations thereof. And when it wasn't ball, it was swimming, wrestling, ice-skating, tennis or fishing. We would even fish in the winter. Chip a hole through foot-thick ice, bait a hook with frost-bitten fingers, drop your line through the hole, and try to keep moving so as not to freeze to the very surface supporting you while waiting for a bite.

My father and mother grew-up in Muskegon, and, after WWII, they moved my three-year-older brother Terry and me to Coral Gables, Florida, ostensibly for Pop to go to dental school at the University of Miami. Dad had attacked Normandy on D-Day, stormed across Europe with Patton and won a battlefield commission along the way. He didn't speak of the war unless he was drunk, and then so sullenly and maudlin that he was scary and made little sense.

Coral Gables was a damned fine place to be a kid. The weather was balmy, stormy or blowy, but never cold. My folks weren't hands-on parents, so we roved and roamed at will like orphans. For all the attention we got from our parents, we were just that: orphans. We swam with sea cows in the canals and were man-o-war stung together in the Atlantic. We fished and we hunted with our BB guns. We constructed huge forts from palmetto fronds, ate lemons, limes, oranges, and grapefruits right off the trees, and we shinnied up palms and consumed the coconuts as if we were Swiss Family Robinson brothers.

During a neighborhood rock fight, I hit a girl named Gretchen in the head and she nearly bled to death. Dad asked if I did it and I said no. He said he would punish me badly (and he could) if I lied, and it would go easier if I 'fessed-up. I 'fessed, learning forever after to pick my lies carefully, because I got punished anyway. After a couple years of idyllic life in this paradise, my parents lost their minds and moved us back to the snow and blow of Muskegon. I attended Irish-Catholic grade and high schools and distinguished myself as the youngest ever alter boy and an able athlete.

Academics were so-so for me, and that was made more palatable as Mom always said she didn't want any eggheads in the family. She didn't get one in me. After high school, I got an athletic scholarship to a Chicago junior college and, following that, a four-year ride to Southern Colorado. I captained each football team as a defensive back. I won an academic post-graduate scholarship to the University of Nevada in Reno, dropped out after one semester and joined the Army as things were getting interesting, and that's what we were supposed to do. After basic training, advanced infantry, infantry OCS, and jungle school, I went on to Vietnam where I served as a rifle platoon leader, initially, then as recon platoon leader in the 2d Bn, 8th Infantry, 1st Cavalry Division, Airmobile.

...Recon would stay out for days in the deepest part of the bush, trying to gather intel on VC and NVA, attempting to pinpoint their bunker complexes and routes of movement. Our mission was to avoid contact and report back to battalion so that they could airlift rifle companies into the area and provoke a confrontation. Or, artillery would blow hell out of infiltration routes that we identified. We frequently walked right into the little bastards, however, and it would hit the fan. Sometimes we could not resist and we would ambush them when we knew their force was small and we could didi out of the AO after the contact and get extracted.

Our group was small so the last thing we ever wanted was to get tangled up with a superior force that could overwhelm us. It happened, though. We never talked and we were real quiet. We were damned good. By 1971, both sides had their blood up and we hated them enough to want to kill as many as we possibly could. Something about those young American kids let them take instinctively to the jungle and its uniquely vicious fighting style. My platoon sergeant had that part of the 23d Psalm that talks about walking through the valley of the shadow of death scripted on his helmet cover. It ended by saying that he didn't fear anything because he was the baddest son of a bitch in the valley. He was. We all were. Maybe that's why we always won in the bush...

Now I know why when Dad got drunk he was sullen and maudlin when he talked about the war. He was just confused. Like me. And like me, he probably never got over the surprise of coming back alive. Or the guilt.

Early Lessons

Bob Flournoy

…hunters move through the field and forest with impunity; they are the only ones with guns. A good hunter will sometimes position himself in a comfortable spot, blending into the environment, and wait for game. He will be aware of the moving air and which direction it carries his scent so that the very wind is his ally. If there is no wind, then he will watch the forest, looking and listening for movement against the stillness. The wind becomes the quarry's friend when it can move with the swaying grass and leaves, and disguise its sound of travel in the background noise of the moving air.

When a hunter is also being hunted by his quarry, a nemesis with a gun instead of fangs, the wind becomes his worst enemy. Millions of years of evolution tell him that those hunting him are using the wind to stalk him silently, swirling their scent, moving with the dance of the trees, careful feet muffled by the noise of the wind. Early humans would take to their caves and trees when the breezes stiffened, nervous and fearful of their silent stalkers. Jungle fighters don't move at all when the wind is up; they hunker down, watch and wait. The highest rates of suicide are in windy places…

And who can ever forget Dizzy Dean. Diz, who, trying to enhance his brother Daffy's contract promised they would win 40 games between them. They won 42 that year, and I believe it was he who first said, "It ain't braggin if you can do it."

Corsicana, Texas, 1950s

Joe Gelineau

Rag arm, termite on the ant hill, duck's on the pond, you throw like a girl (that was the ultimate insult). You could not break a pane-glass window with that, your fastball hits the ground (from gravity) before it reaches the plate. You pitching softball? What pitch was that? Your drop? Your mother teach you how to throw? Try the other arm, that your change-up? Hey batta, batta! Hey ump, you're missing a great game! You couldn't catch a cold shortstop!

Little League baseball was the most powerfully formative experience of my pre-adolescent youth. I remember waiting restless, sleepless nights for the tryouts to begin in early March. You were eligible if you were male and between nine to twelve years on or before a magic date in summer, maybe it was August 31 or end of summer. The wind blew hard in central Texas in March and there were days when the temperature and wind combined to render seemingly unplayable conditions, but we practiced daily at every available chance in those days leading up to the tryouts. It seemed the whole town would know just who was trying out that year and which teams wanted whom and you prayed that you would make the team which had your cousin as the starting pitcher, or which went undefeated last summer, or any team at all.

Getting picked up was one thing, not getting cut in the first two weeks was another. If you made the team, hats were next. Every day the coach would hand out a hat the color of the team you would play on, either Reds, Greens, Blues, Maroons, Blacks or Oranges, with felt emblem, in our case letters A for American league or N for National league, to be attached to the front. Coach handed out a single hat to the player who hustled or improved, or bunted, or slid best that day. Wearing that hat the next day to school, after shaping it all night with rubber bands around the brim to curve it and ironing the crease, was a heraldic moment which never went unnoticed in the hallways and playgrounds.

I will always remember my tryout. I was a big nine-year-old, having turned in early September the year before, just after the cutoff. I had to ride my bike over to Sam Houston Elementary, one of four public elementary schools named famously for Robert E. Lee, James Bowie, and W.B. Travis, where tryouts were staged on the recess fields. I went to the Parochial school, Immaculate Conception; no tryouts held there, so I rode furiously the several miles to Sam Houston, afraid I would miss it and my destiny to play in Little League Baseball.

They had pulled up a panel truck with a PA system and were organized to the extent that hitting events and fielding events were all announced and tryout players called out by name. Waiting breathlessly along the fenced area by the backstop, I was approached by a blonde kid, 10 or 11 years old and cocky, with a catcher's mitt, accompanied by a stocky intense man who introduced himself as Mr. Pierce. He explained that he was the coach of the American Reds and asked if I would pitch to his catcher Winston Weaver, or Winnie. I nodded my assent, spit on the ground, and began to throw the ball into Winnie's mitt. No curves or junk, just straight fast balls, he said. As the pitches found their target, Winnie shook his head and Mr. Pierce grinned and said thanks and that he would be watching for me in the tryout drills.

Later they called out, "Buddy Gelineau, third base," and I ran out onto the diamond as fast as I ever had before. The instructions were to field a ground ball and throw it to first, simple. The bat cracked and the skinner came hard to my left. I moved left and forward, scooping the ball up and in one continuous motion, leveled a strike in the first baseman's chest. My head was swimming, but I knew I had delivered. The PA truck declared, "That's a nine year old."

I made the American Reds that spring and went on to play four years as a shortstop and relief pitcher. I learned more in those years from Chuck Pierce, Winnie, Carrots, Hughie, Tom Wilson, Phil Pascal, and all my team mates than I thought ever possible. Coach Pearce called me "Ce' vas," pronounced Savah, because my Mom taught French lessons to some of us kids. Oh, to go back to Stuart Bebe Field for one more summer night.

Things Are Never as They Seem

Bob Flournoy, III

As a young boy, sitting quietly at the dinner table at our family's old farmhouse, listening to the stories my parents, aunts, uncles and grandparents there was a wealth of folk and family lore during dinner and the idle time after in front of the fire. With no television and unreliable radio reception in rural Alabama of the 1950s, we practiced the age-old but now fading art of just plain talking. As a result of those moments, I can appreciate the passing down of stories in ancient cultures that did not have the written word. I also understand how, over time, younger generations, completely spellbound and enthralled by these stories, could and did slowly change the tone and content of what they had heard. I have never retold the story of Pete Redi, but it has festered in my mind over the years, growing from the seed of conversation that was planted in my subconscious around that old dinner table so many years ago.

Pete came with his bride, Lotti, to the college in Auburn, Alabama, in 1946, after WWII, on the GI bill to study electrical engineering. He had been a POW in Germany at the end of the war, crashing his P51 Mustang in occupied Holland in 1944. My dad had flown in the China/Burma/India theater and was at Auburn with his young wife (and me) for the same reason. They wore their old uniforms to class, as that was about the extent of their wardrobes, and, recognizing one another as brothers of the Army Air Corps, they

"JUST A LITTLE RAIN..."

became fast friends. We were in luck to have such wonderful people come into our lives, and the Redis were in luck because my grand parents had a farm outside Auburn where hungry young students would always be fed. This was the setting of many memorable tales from those days, told around that dinner table in the quiet of rural Alabama nights. One particular story would haunt me my entire life and come to an astounding conclusion almost 50 years later.

In March of 1944, Lt. Pete Redi was flying his P51 fighter out of Germany toward the English Channel, accompanied by his wingman and commanding officer, Captain Paul Zimmer. They were flying high and tight when they saw a lone German fighter down below them. Capt. Paul gave the order and they dove to attack this target of opportunity, too late to realize that he was a decoy for a half dozen German fighters high in the clouds with the sun to their backs. Down they came and all hell broke loose, Pete and Paul vastly outnumbered by a foe with the edge of altitude. Almost immediately, a cannon shot from an ME109 exploded in Pete's cockpit and he blacked out with a vague memory of enemy planes swarming around him and a fast departing wingman as he fled upward and homeward, leaving him to his fate. Regaining consciousness as his P51 was angling toward the ground at treetop level, Pete managed to roll out of the airplane and attempt to open his chute. The partially opened parachute caught in the branches of a very large tree, and broke his fall just enough to save his life, but did not save his leg, which broke upon impact.

In a fog of pain and confusion, he witnessed his aircraft impact in a farmer's field 100 yards away and explode in a bright fireball as he passed out. When he opened his eyes, he saw the distant speck of his wingman's P51 racing west across the English Channel. He became aware that he was in the yard of a small, rural farmhouse, and watched a young boy and girl, who turned out to be brother and sister, approach him from the house. They were accompanied by an older man, who turned out to be their father. They laid him on a table in the old house to see if they could give him medical help. Very quickly, the house was full of people from neighboring farms who had witnessed the crash. This was a notable event in rural Holland, and they came from all around to see the 20-year-old American flyer. As various men and women in the crowded little house attempted to administer medical help to Pete, the gestapo, who had witnessed the event also, arrived on the scene and took custody of Pete, taking him away toward an unknown fate, and out of the lives of those farmers as quickly as he had entered.

Pete was kept in isolation, his wounds unattended for several days. Cold, hungry and in pain, he was finally taken before a German officer who spoke perfect English and, as it turned out, had attended college in the U.S. Cordially offering him a cigarette and speaking in a soft voice, the German placed a dossier in front of Pete on the small wooden table at which he sat and instructed him to read through it. His words were something to the affect that there should not be any bullshit passed between them because there really was very little that the German military did not already know about him. Astounded, Pete leafed through the papers, reading newspaper articles about himself enlisting in the Army air corps and graduating from flight school.

German intelligence had been working hard in the United States long before Pete, or for that matter the country itself, entered World War II. Deflated somewhat, Pete listened quietly to the questions of Hitler's master race representative, attentive to the fact that he had information that this polite man wanted. In a nutshell, the German wanted to know who gave the order for the P51 pilots to eject the extra fuel pods that they carried. These pods enabled the fighters to do something that American fighters had never been able to do before; accompany their bombers all the way to the target and back. German strategy was to attack the bomber formation over the target with their own fighters, hoping to disrupt the accuracy of the bomb run. When that attack began, the P51's would eject their now empty fuel pods in order to maneuver and fight the enemy defenders. Still with a full-on-board fuel supply, they could accomplish this task and still make it back to England. Had the German fighters gone after the bomber formation when it entered the European continent, the P51's would have let their almost full pods go in order to dogfight the enemy, and they would not have had enough fuel to continue to the target deep in mainland Germany, leaving the American bomber fleet vulnerable and unprotected. But, uncharacteristically, the Germans never figured this out and never changed their strategy.

Sensing what his interrogator was trying to discern, Pete gave him an answer that was perfectly acceptable to a German military man. "I am just a lowly lieutenant. I eject the fuel pod when my captain tells me to." Having satisfied his inquisitor, Lt. Redi was sent on to a stalag in remote northern Germany, where he spent the next 13 months listening to the V2 rockets being launched toward England from a nearby missile base, wrestling with his impressions of how his wingman had handled the encounter with the German fighters.

Capt. Paul, in the meantime, had returned to his base in England and reported that Lt. Redi's plane had crashed, and that there was a fireball and no parachute. It was a reasonable assumption that Pete was KIA. Life and the war went on, and Pete was counted as one of the many who had died. It would be six months before the Red Cross caught up to Pete in the POW camp and notify his fiancée, Lotti, that he was, in fact, alive. Capt. Paul never got that word, and it would be 50 years before he finally did. That 50-year journey would culminate in revelations both unexpected and joyous for all. It would have a monumental impact on all of us who had spent those many years angry at Capt. Paul Zimmer for having committed that most unforgivable of sins: deserting a fellow comrade in arms in the face of the enemy.

Lotti, of course, was wild with the joy of receiving news that her fiancé was alive after living with a heavy heart for six months. There are many stories about that time, and the remainder of the 13 months that Pete spent as a POW. Hilarious, heartbreaking, unimaginable stories of his life as a POW and finally being liberated by the Russians are a book in themselves, but would detract from our focus on Capt. Paul's lack of action in defense of his friend and wingman. We need heroes in our lives, and we need to balance their deeds and principles with antagonists. It is our nature as humans to establish clear opposites to measure our behavior against, whether in mythology, parables from the bible or whatever religious theology we have chosen. There is good and there is evil, and in this saga our families had their hero and villain.

In 1995, the 8th Air Force, which had ravaged Germany from the air during the war, held its 50th reunion in England. Thousands of pilots attended, aging men returning to relive those brief shining moments in their lives when they had been all that they ever could or hope to be. War offers that opportunity. It is a sobering fact that we measure ourselves as men by how we behaved as kids in those deadly hours. That has never changed, not since early man picked up a club and advanced alongside his fellow tribesmen against a perceived threat. My own rich life of family and friends is, in many respects, the product of my service with an infantry company in Vietnam. Such was the case when Pete returned to reunite with his friends of old. He went on a whim, and when he and Lotti decided to rent a car and tour the lowlands of the continent after the reunion, also on a whim, events were set in motion that were being unbelievably paralleled in the United States by their son, Bob, unbeknownst to anyone.

Being a man of detail, besides love for his father, Bob Redi had begun, some years before, to chronicle the life of his father. When the Freedom of Information Act opened the records and files of so many to anyone who had the gumption to dig into the tangled web of government records, Bob began to research his dad's military career. He retrieved his files and opened the vault of detailed information that outlined the almost daily happenings of Pete from 1943 until he exited the service in 1945. Every order, every award and every duty assignment was there before him. Most intriguing were the fascinating after-action reports that had been filed by Pete and his constituents after every mission flown out of England over 50 years ago. It was in one of these documents that he discovered the report filed by Capt. Zimmer that detailed his father's "death" and the events that had occurred during that last encounter with the enemy. It contained some astonishing revelations concerning the dogfight and Capt. Paul's part in it. It also pointed Bob in another unexpected direction—researching the records and life of Pete's old commanding officer—a journey that would reinforce the age-old adage that things are never simple and seldom as they seem. With his research complete, a contemplative Bob Redi went in search of his father's old friend.

"JUST A LITTLE RAIN..."

As Bob was about his task, researching his father and his father's old CO, Pete and Lotti were on a carefree bright summer sojourn in an automobile that they had rented, taking the opportunity of being in England for the reunion to sight-see on the mainland. They found themselves driving through the countryside of rural Holland one day and, in one of those slow motion moments that occur in all of our lives, one of those little windows that tie things together in our individual universes, Pete had the chilling feeling that he was in a place of special meaning and content. Stopping the car on a quiet country road, Pete quietly pointed out the window to an enormous old tree that stood in the yard of a little cottage, and told Lotti that he believed it to be the tree that had snagged his streaming parachute and slowed his plunge to the ground, sparing his life so long ago. With his skeptical wife sitting beside him, he drove into the yard and slowly got out of the car, looking around.

A couple in their late fifties or early sixties emerged from the house and stared at Pete, a 5'5" tall distinctively craggy faced man whom one would never forget and, with a cry and a shout, the brother and sister who had tended to him over 50 years ago ran to him. In stunned disbelief, he was led into the little house by the joyous couple who were speaking to him a mile a minute in broken English. As they led him into the only large room, Pete saw before him the wooden table that he had been laid upon so long ago. As he gazed about, speechless, words from a very old man's voice came out of the shadows behind him, "How's your leg, son?"

Word quickly spread in the small Dutch farming community that the "American boy" who had brought such excitement to their village so long ago and had become something of a legend since, had returned. People flocked in from surrounding farms, food and beer were produced and the unbelievable reunion grew into a celebration, with all present who had been on the scene so long ago competing with one another to tell their version of those distant events as they remembered them. One man, who was 57 years old and had witnessed from a neighboring farm the entire confrontation with the Germans from start to finish, praised Pete exuberantly for his aircraft maneuvering and fighter-pilot skills, recounting in detail the dog fight that had roared above those farms and fields, ending in the explosions of two enemy aircraft high above, while the others fled to the east. Pete opened his mouth to inform this man that his memories as a seven-year-old were not accurate, and that he, Pete, had taken a hit the moment the conflict began, which resulted in his crash. He stopped as it dawned on him what he was hearing—the truth—after all these years. The young boy had been watching Capt. Paul.

Many months after he began his quest for the faceless Capt. Paul, Bob was able to track him to San Diego, California. Paul had long ago left his home of record in Maine, and had moved several times. With a fair amount of luck, destiny perhaps, Bob had stumbled onto the phone number of Paul's old hometown boyhood minister as he searched for the lost trail. Even nine years ago the internet was not a tool for such research as it is now, so the task was daunting. After hearing Bob's story and motives for desiring to make contact, the old preacher gave Bob the elusive phone number that was to complete the circle that took a half century to travel.

The telephone rang in a home in San Diego one evening, and an old woman answered. She informed the caller that General Zimmer was out for the evening but would be available the next night. Mrs. Zimmer asked if she could take a message, and she did; Bob Redi was calling and would like to speak with her husband. He would call the following day. When he did, the same old voice answered and, when Bob identified himself, she informed Bob that her husband was looking forward to his call, but to be aware of the fact that the general was old and in bad health, and that he had been in an extreme state of nervous anticipation since he had gotten Bob's message. When he came on the phone, Bob asked him if he knew who he was.

The old voice said, "Yes, son, I know who you are, and I would like to say something before we go any further." He began to tell Bob all of the things that Bob already knew, except one. "I flew 300 combat missions in WWII, Korea and Vietnam. I flew P51's in WWII, F86's in Korea and F4 Phantoms in Vietnam. They are all a blur to me now, and I remember few, if any, details of any of them as single events, with the exception of the mission that took the life of your father. I loved him dearly and I have never forgiven myself for giving the order to attack that German plane, as we were almost home, and I should have seen the trap that had been laid. We were at war and our job was to kill German planes, so that is what I gave the command to do. But it has grieved me for these many years and the image of your father's exploding plane has haunted me since."

Bob quietly and gently told the old man what had actually happened and the joyful response that he received would warm his heart for a lifetime.

They talked at length, and Bob promised to get the general and his dad connected. The old man had never suspected that he had been so wrongly judged and condemned, and Bob could not wait to tell his dad, who was, at that moment, in Holland. He was burning with the truth that he had discovered while researching the war records of both men, especially the revealing after action report of that fateful mission that had haunted them both for so long. Little did he know that Pete was discovering the same truth half a world away, from a man who, as a child, had seen the events unfold before his very eyes. But, just before he bade the old general goodbye, he spoke these words to him…

"*General, I noticed while researching your records that you were credited with downing four enemy aircraft in the three wars that you fought in; one in WWII, two in Korea and one in Vietnam. You needed one more to reach the total of five required for ACE status. I also noticed that in your after-action report, you claimed to have shot down two German fighters in the skies above my dad's burning aircraft, but only one could be verified. Well, sir, I have an eye-witness that you did indeed shoot down two enemy planes that day. I know my dad will be pleased to know that you are an ACE.*"

And so began Bob's next project, a simple one compared to what he had been faced with in the previous months of research to discover the truth; a statement from a Dutch farmer would be a fitting capstone to General Paul Zimmer's career.

Just before the old general died, he did, in fact, link up with Pete on the phone. He passed away before they could arrange a face to face reunion. But high in the mountains of North Carolina, where the Redis have a summer home, there are many visitors from a small Dutch farming community on a regular basis; I can see the big grin on Pete's face. I now know that Pete never truly believed that his friend had betrayed him. It was "us" that needed a villain to prove our loyalty to him. He, however, knew long ago what we all should learn sooner than later… one never goes wrong when he resists the urge to judge and instead gives the nod to love, because then there is never a need to forgive. And that is the lesson that a young boy finally learned, after all these years.

Jacksonville, North Carolina, 1950s-60s

Mike King

Running home, hot and sweaty, open field moves between billowing sheets of laundry, drying in the unfenced back yards of neighbors who had carports with pink Nashes and Buicks. You had better be in the house before dark but there was time to stop in the back of a house, any house, and drink from their hose or faucet, long draughts of cool sweet water.

When I was six years old, we moved into a new house in an entirely new development that was being carved out of what used to be a dairy farm. Lots of fields, large trees, a couple of creeks and a man-made lake of about 200 acres meandered through this property. Like a lot of people in the early fifties, my parents were both veterans of military service and took advantage of V.A. loans to achieve the American dream of owning a house. We were the first foundation in the entire development and my parents live in this house to this day.

As a kid, this was a perfect setting. Summers were spent tormenting anything that moved with a BB gun. Especially lizards and frogs, but the prey of high value was any sort of snakes which were plentiful in the coastal low country of North Carolina. Houses began to spring up at a fairly good pace and soon we had a neighborhood with many kids our age, and this made reptilian life forms almost endangered in our little area. Of course, we were told repeatedly, "Do not go near that lake," which was only about 200 yards from my house. There had to be something good there to be reminded almost daily not to overstep. Of course we went-daily. In addition to lizards and frogs, there were terrapin turtles in abundance, usually sunning on some deadfall or stumps that poked up a few inches from the surface of the water, that at one time were large trees before the lake. Fishing was also in the mill as this lake was full of bluegills, shiners and largemouth bass. But the main activity of summer was baseball. Several times a day and a great deal of my summer childhood was spent carving out a place to play from the myriad of fields around our house. These ball fields lasted until someone would decide to build a house, and then we would start over again.

When I was about six or seven, we got about 24 baby ducks one Easter. They were little yellow fuzz balls, but quickly grew into the classic white duck. After a few weeks, we decided to set them free, and the lake was the ideal setting. The descendants of these ducks still reside there to this day. A year or so later, my brother and I became the proud owners of two puppies. Both were about six to eight weeks old. One was a German Shepard that we named Zip. The other was a hybrid of some sort that grew into a perfectly scaled, 25 pound replica of a black lab. This one we dubbed Wompi, thinking this was a great Native American sounding name. Although Wompi was short in stature, he possessed a great zest for life.

As we grew, the lake and creeks became a part of the daily life of our dogs and ourselves. This opened a chapter in the life of Wompi that I will never forget. During our daily excursions to the lake, Wompi discovered our ducks. He wanted one badly and I am not certain he knew why, but it was embedded in his genetic fabric. The one drawback to his grand scheme of things was that he, like many dogs, hated water. His forays were confined to chasing them from the banks whenever he got near, but he never caught a duck. This, however, did not dampen his spirits. One spring, things changed. The ducks nested every spring. Most would select a spot on one of the

"JUST A LITTLE RAIN…"

stumps through the lake that provided dry habitat, with grasses and weeds around the stumps for cover. Some of the ducks were a little slow of learning though. They would select a nesting site along the banks in the tall grass and bull rushes. These slow learners became the objects of Wompi's intense interest.

Several times a day, Wompi would wander down to the lake to try his luck at catching the ducks who now seemed to spend much more time close to dry land. In these days, there were no leash laws and our dogs were free to roam the neighborhood. Wompi would head to the lake and torment the bank nesters. This would go on for a week or so before the nesting pairs would give up and abandon the nest. Several days after this exodus, the fun began. Wompi now discovered that there was something in these nests that had been left behind and it interested him to no end. After a few days in the sun, these "items" became very ripe. Wompi must have relished the scent, because he would just roll and wallow in these now abandoned and extremely smelly duck eggs. As if this were not bad enough, he would then come strutting proudly home.

You could see him coming and it seemed to me that there were lines emanating from him, much like the heat induced distortions one sees from mirages on the Sahara desert. I do not know what it was about this scent that made him happy, but he walked proudly. Once he entered our domain, we would pounce on him. There were still egg shells and yellow yolk dried to his coat. We would promptly take him to the back yard and hose him down and douse him with dishwashing soap. As I stated, he did not like this forced water ritual and immediately, upon being released from this torture, he would roll in the dirt anywhere he could. Although he smelled better, he seemed less happy. This ritual would continue every spring for about 12 years until Wompi finally gave this practice up. I could not tell if he just tired of the chase or hated the forced bathing. I personally believe it was the baths.

Always thankful that there was no rain on the weekend, I remember every kid in our neighborhood showing up at some vacant field with two-foot-high weeds, lawnmower in hand, and we would set about making a new field. We had visions of a smaller version of

Yankee Stadium with cut-out base paths, grass infield, etc., but after four hours or so it was time to play. Clumps of weeds or grass would send any ground ball in random directions. Backstop was a couple of poles and chicken wire. Over the days, the field would be reduced to bare ground from the traffic and it would remain the daily gathering spot, until one day builders would show up to build a house and the process repeated itself somewhere else.

Once in a while, we would all get on our bikes (go anywhere in my hometown on a bike and if you misbehaved, this news would find its way to your parents before you got home) and head for the Little League field. It had a fence, backstop, dugouts and all the trappings of a "real field." Mostly, we frequented the home-grown field several times a day during the summer. Sometimes the carving out of a new field yielded surprises, like a covey of quail, or raccoons and, if you were lucky, Copperheads! They did not last long. Bats can be used for many things. Speaking of which, bats were a precious commodity. My dad was a Little League coach and he would bring home all of the broken bats (only wood was used in those days). We would hammer in a few small nails and add electrical tape and the bat would find new life. Baseballs were also sometimes taped up with electrical tape until someone would show up with a new ball.

To choose up sides, we had a ritual where one player threw a bat straight up into the air and another caught it. He had to keep his grip where he caught it and the other kid would grip the bat just above him—hands had to touch. They would alternate hand over hand to the bottom of the bat. When it became semi-obvious who might win when you got close to the knob, you could also fork. That is, instead of gripping the bat with your entire hand, you could spread your index and middle finger and place the bat between them while still touching the hand of the previous gripper. It got complicated, but in the end it was just as you described—the person who could hold the knob and throw the bat got first choice from the talent pool. You could also become quite good at catching the bat in the correct place such that you had the best chance of winning. Watch the Louisville Slugger label. It must have been a universal practice passed from generation to generation.

"JUST A LITTLE RAIN..."

Sometimes we did not have enough players for an actual game, so we spent hours playing 500. This game involved a batter hitting fly balls toward the mob assembled in center field. If someone caught a fly ball, it was worth 100 points if the catcher could throw a ball toward home plate and hit a bat laid on the ground at home plate, 90 degrees to the direction of the thrown ball. The hitter could not touch the bat. One-hop ground balls were 75 points, two-hop ground balls were 50 points and, in each instance, you had to hit the bat. In the event that you did hit the bat, if the batter caught the ball after it jumped from the bat before it hit the ground, the points were negated. The best luck involved hitting the bat and having the ball just bounce back toward the outfield. As you can see, the batter had a distinct advantage and it sometimes took more than one session to take the bat from him. There was also a jungle rules in the outfield. A fly ball was like a pass thrown up for interception. It was fair game for everyone with lots of "jockeying" for position. Any missed fly or ground ball was zero points.

At other times, when we had less than two full sides, we would play shorthanded with certain parts of the field off limits. If we only had enough for two infielders and two outfielders, anything hit to the right of second base, either on the ground or in the air, was an automatic out. The game went on. Other variations involved using a tennis ball. Same game, but different ball. We tried golf balls as well and even nine-year-olds could hit a golf ball with a bat at a considerable distance. Ground balls hit at someone were a different matter entirely. Even we concluded that the golf ball game was full of risks and we abandoned it, but not until actual blood had been drawn on several occasions.

One attempt at finding a plot for a new field led us to an old structure that had long ago been abandoned. I could not describe it, but it had some old gutter down-spouts that were splitting open. Further investigation led to the discovery that this down-spout was inhabited! The dwellers were bats (the flying kind)! Bats were fair game in my world. We hauled out of there and returned with several cans of lighter fluid and matches. We doused the down-spout with as much as we could squirt and fired it up. We could hear scratching sounds and then the exodus began. Bats flying in broad daylight, and kids scrambling in every direction at high rates of speed. We had no idea of what danger bats could bring, but we did not stay around to find out. It was exhilarating. This plot, however, did not become the home of our next ball field.

In my part of the world, Little League was sacred. There were eight teams with 15 boys per team. Age group was from 9-12 (you could not be 13 before the first of August in order to be eligible to play). To prevent teams from consisting of only 12-year-olds, there was a requirement for each team to have at least two nine-year-olds, three ten-year-olds and no more than five in any age group. Therefore, most teams were as I described; two nine-year-olds, three ten-year-olds, five eleven-year-olds and five twelve-year-olds. We played about 20 games a year, usually two per week on Monday, Wednesday, and Friday evenings, with the second game under the lights. First game started at 5:30 p.m.

Tryouts were a week long and each person wanting to try out was assigned a number on a piece of thick paper and it was safety pinned to his shirt. You were to bring this number with you every day of tryouts. This allowed coaches to identify who they may be interested in drafting and they actually held a draft. Everyone who did not make a Little League team was relegated to the recreation-department-sponsored league or, as we used to refer to it, the Minor Leagues. Wearing a hat from a Little League team was a badge of honor and you were never without one during the entire summer. Of course, you could only wear the hat you had last year as the current year's caps were reserved for games only. This made the hats more sacred, as it implied you had made the team at least two years. You were a bonafide stud.

During tryouts, we were all lined up and coaches put us through various drills. I do not remember the total number of folks who came out, but if you got through a single drill during a day, you were lucky. There must have been thousands, although reality is that it was probably 100 or 150. During the fourth day of tryouts, I was horsing around on top of a dugout with a friend and he pushed me off. I fell on my left arm and broke the bone in my upper arm. This effectively ended my season, or so I thought. I would go to the games anyway with my left arm in a cast. It was six weeks before I got my cast off and at one of the games a coach I did not know asked my dad if I was cleared to play. When told yes, he disappeared and came back with a uniform and the prized cap. I was "drafted" by the Chamber of Commerce team, as they had saved a place for me.

Our colors were white with green trim. We also had teams sponsored by the Lions, American Legion, Moose, Jaycees, Kiwanis, Rotary, and VFW. Being one of two teams blessed with letters that were easily transformed into a slur (CC for Chamber of Commerce and AL for American Legion), we were lovingly referred to as the Commode Cleaners. Bad, but not as bad as the AL (Ass Lickers). I remember my very first at bat. We were not the best team in the league and we were playing the Moose, who were. Mainly due to a single guy named Mike Genshaw. He was about 6'2" and weighed 180 (I may be wrong here, but he was a legend). He was pitching and I was inserted into the game in the fourth inning after we were already behind by about ten runs.

In those days, we played by major league rules; once you were taken out of the game, you were out for good. I was inserted into right field, the last position on any team and where you always placed your weakest player. I got through the inning without incident and I led off the inning as the batter. Genshaw was pitching and he threw about 110 mph; I am certain. I grabbed the shortest bat I could find (29 inches) and choked up to almost the label and made up my mind that I would swing on the first pitch and start that swing at about the time Genshaw started his windup so as not to be late. I closed my eyes and made solid contact, looked up and saw a line drive right past the first baseman (I was hitting right handed and thought I had started swinging early) into right field for a hit. I stopped at first base and was scared to death. That was as far as I got, too, as the other three batters were retired without my having to leave the bag. I was substituted for and left the game, but I got a hit off the most dominant baseball player I had ever seen. And it was my very first at bat in a sanctioned game of any kind. I will remember that forever; so will my dad.

Remember Dizzy Dean talking about catfish he had caught in the off season in Mississippi? Bragging about nine-inch catfish. Finally, Pee Wee asked him what was so great about catching a nine-inch catfish. Dizzy says, "Pee Wee, the nine inches was the distance between the eyes." Pee Wee was smart enough not to fall for Dizzy's bait often, but every now and then, ol' Diz got him.

Mike King, 1958

A Different Slant on Things

Mike King

...As a son of the South, growing up in the 50s and 60s, I was imbued with some of the subtle facets of Southern culture. Some of this has held me in good stead over my lifetime and other parts have been a lifetime in culling from my gene pool. The south, in general, is permeated with patriotism. This may not be any stronger than in other pockets of the United States, but as a geographical region, it is very widespread. When I entered the US Army in June of 1969, after receiving my commission from West Point, the Vietnam war was in full swing. I was commissioned a second lieutenant in the Field Artillery and, after the usual schools for new officers, I was stationed in Schweinfurt, Germany for my first assignment.

I immediately became a Battery Executive Officer and four months later, after having been promoted to first lieutenant three weeks earlier, I became the Battery Commander of a 155 mm Self Propelled Howitzer Battery. Command slots are highly sought after by career military officers, so tenure was usually a year in length. After 16 months in this slot, it became obvious that my time in command of a battery was about up and the alternative was some slot on the battalion staff. This was not very appealing to me, so my culture intervened and I volunteered for duty in Vietnam. This was in September of 1971, and the war effort was winding down as the US population had tired of seeing the war in their living rooms every night. My thinking was not all gung-ho as I had heard that many folks were getting as far as the US and then being reassigned as the number of folks needed in a contracting that war was waning.

As is often the case, this turned out to be a rumor that was not substantiated by one ounce of fact. So, on February 18, 1972, I found myself standing on the tarmac at Travis AFB at 0500 waiting to board a charter Stretch DC 8 bound for Saigon. By the way, there was not an empty seat on the entire aircraft. We made stops in Anchorage, Alaska, and Yokota, Japan. After the three-hour layover in Yokota, we re-boarded the aircraft and there was now a total of five passengers comprised of myself and four helicopter pilot warrant officers. The crew on the DC 8 was bigger than the passenger load. Next stop: Long Binh, Vietnam.

We stayed with the 90th replacement battalion in Long Binh for three days awaiting assignment to a unit and transportation to wherever we were going. The 90th was also an out-processing center for those who had served their time in country and were going home. These departing souls were the source of some of the greatest graffiti I have ever seen. The walls of the entire 90th replacement complex should have been preserved and reconstructed in the US as an example of the true nature of that conflict. Poetry, art, irony, and sarcasm were on display in the highest unedited form. It was truly amazing.

I was finally assigned to the 196th Infantry Brigade in Da Nang, up north. By this time, there were two units of the US Army still functioning in Vietnam. The 196th, in Da Nang, and a brigade of the 1st Cavalry operating around Saigon and parts west. We made it as far as Cam Rahn Bay on the first leg of our flight up country. As is typical with any military operation, we had only been manifested this far and it took us another four days to get to Da Nang. During this layover in Cam Rahn Bay, we were rocketed three nights and there was a sapper attack on the Army side of the base, although we were nowhere near that event.

I began to wonder what the hell I had gotten myself into and why was I stupid enough to volunteer for this. We finally made Da Nang and I was assigned as S-3 of a battalion. My stay with the 196th proved to be short lived, however, and in June of '72, the last two US Army ground units left in Vietnam were disbanded and USARV ceased to exist as a command. There was roughly a battalion-sized unit from each brigade left behind to pull air field security as there were still F-4s flying over the north from Da Nang airfield and still air support missions flown out of Thon Son Nhut air field near Saigon. This was all very exciting, as there was a chance that I was going to go home only after four months in country.

While with the 196th, I did get the opportunity to see some things that I had only ever read about. I flew C&C for a 121 vehicle convoy from Da Nang to Phu Bai, which was way up north. That had been a part of the 101st when they occupied that part of the country. This convoy route took us over the Hai Van pass and along the "street without joy" more commonly called QL 1. We offloaded a lot of material for the MACV teams and some little known sites that were used for listening to radio traffic. We did not ask who they were and we were not told. On another occasion, we flew aerial recon out of one of our fire bases (by this time, we only occupied two with the single battalion of artillery left in the 196th) and had the opportunity to fly over the Ashau Valley, an ominous looking place that had claimed many American lives over the previous seven years.

In June 1972, the American stand down began with full force. We spent the better part of several weeks turning in equipment as part of the shrinking force structure. Rumors were of all varieties and plentiful. As it turned out, one of my classmates and I were reassigned to MACV teams. I thought this was a little strange as the 196th had been receiving members from MACV teams for weeks, as they were also standing down. My friend Sam was assigned to MACV Team 36 in Pleiku and I was assigned to MACV Team 46 in Khanh Hoa Province. I was the only Artillery advisor in all of Military Region II. Vietnam was divided into four regions by the US Military and they were called Corps. I Corps was in the north and IV Corps was the southern most region. The names were changed from Corps to Regions sometime before I became MACV. Team 46 operated five district teams and the HQ element located in Nha Trang and all of this was in Military Region II.

MACV teams consisted of both Civil Operations and Military Operations. The CivOps side was mainly staffed with Foreign Service Officers from the Department of State and the MilOps staff came from the US Army. All team components outside of Nha Trang were MilOps. As the Artillery Advisor, I had eleven two-gun mini fire bases throughout the province. Twenty of these tubes were M101, 105 mm Howitzers and two tubes were towed 155 mm howitzers, commonly called pigs. I was also the S-2 Advisor, the S-3 Advisor and the Senior Regional Force/Popular Force Advisor (called Ruff Puffs). We had 35 RF companies and 125 PF platoons throughout the province and no ARVN troops. The RFs were more like regular Army units and the PFs were more like reservists that were on weekend duty everyday. That is to say they were not as well trained or equipped as the RF units and their duties were mainly relegated to protecting assets such as bridges. The RF units were actively engaged in combat operations on a daily basis.

I finally arrived at MACV Team 46 in June of '72, after rotating through headquarters in Saigon and visiting several teams within Military Region II. I shared a hooch with a Captain Dan, who is now a Major General and who was on his second tour in Vietnam when I met him. He was an Armor officer and had spent his first tour with an armor unit and had been awarded the Silver Star.

By October, I was well entrenched into MACV Team 46. One morning in October, Dan frantically came waking me, as he was the duty officer. We had an RF company hit with a mortar attack and within a few minutes there were 34 KIA and almost everyone else was wounded. They had chosen a night position that was almost 400 meters from where they had reported. Rather than occupy a position in the wood line and fight bugs, snakes and whatever else, they had chosen a site in the middle of rice paddies that housed a pagoda and a few other small structures that were elevated above the paddies by about six feet. Of course, this was easy to pinpoint on a map and easier yet to target with mortars, and that is what happened. Dan and I hit the road before light and headed to the site near our district of Ninh Hoa. There was also a ninth ROK compound in this district, but they were not a part of our charter. When the mortar attack took place, they had figured that reinforcements would come from a nearby RF company, and the plan was to ambush them before they could reinforce. This ambush was never sprung and, as a result, the VC elements who launched the mortar attack were left defenseless, trying to exfiltrate across about four kilometers of rice paddies. I flew C&C for the artillery and we had Cobras flying from the ninth ROK teams using flachette rockets or nails, as they were lovingly called. What ensued was nothing short of wholesale murder. The Cobras rolled on the VC in the open of the rice paddies and the artillery cut off all escape routes. When it was all over, we had confirmed KIA of over 100 and all sorts of mortars, ammunition, survivors and maps. It was from this day that I have memories that will forever be etched in my brain.

First, I witnessed a survivor being interrogated by the RVN. This survivor was shot up badly and it was obvious that he would not live without some immediate medical attention by a surgeon. The Vietnamese interrogators thrust map after map in front of him and yelled all sorts of commands and threats at him for over two hours, until he died. One of them then kicked the guy in disgust, he having died without giving enough information. It became painfully clear to me that there was not one ounce of compassion in the makeup of the South Vietnamese military. None. An absolute absence of anything but disgust for the enemy. It did occur to me that they had been fighting this war all their lives, but it was a startling revelation in my mind.

Of course, the NVA had no compassion for the south once they ended the whole affair, killing too many to count. So much for surrender. But late that afternoon, we began moving wounded and dead out of the area by a three-quarter-ton ambulance. It was a drive of about six kilometers up a dirt road from the CP to the site. This road was raised about four feet above the surrounding ground, which had been cleared of any vegetation taller than six inches out to 50-75 meters on either side of the road. I was driving a jeep into the site that I had only seen from the air up to this point. I had a Major who was the district advisor and who was on his third tour in Vietnam. In 1968 he had been at Hue and was nominated for the Medal of Honor and received the Distinguished Service Cross. We also had two interpreters in the back with weapons out each side of the jeep.

We came up behind a three-quarter-ton ambulance moving at a slow pace. There was no room to pass, so we followed. This ambulance then disappeared before my eyes in a loud noise and a cloud of dust. My jeep also nose-dived down and we halted, violently. The ambulance had hit an improvised 105 mm artillery shell that was obviously on some sort of crude timing device just below the road surface. It blew the ambulance off the road and killed both passengers. Our jeep was blasted with grit and debris from the explosion, which also perforated the radiator, flattened both front tires and crystallized the windshield. This created an explosion of glass fragments and they peppered my arms and the Major's arms with countless small glass fragments. Both the Major and I were sent to the dispensary and field hospital complex in Nha Trang to have the glass removed and to sterilize the wounds to prevent infection. We both declined any thought of purple hearts; too many had paid larger prices for theirs.

It was while we were spending the night in Nha Trang that I met another of my classmates in the dispensary. He had the distinct misfortune of being close enough to a 60 mm mortar explosion that a fragment became embedded right in the heart of man-land—his penis. He was also staying for several days after having this fragment removed. Around midnight on that first night, there we were, talking in the dispensary when a very large, female Major Nurse began asking what the hell we were doing and what we were there for. Berney slowly removed the small filtered cigar that we was smoking and asked me if he should tell her. I smiled my encouragement. She asked again where he had been wounded and he nonchalantly answered, "In the dick." She promptly left without saying another word.

The Paris Peace Accords, which were supposed to end hostilities in Vietnam, took effect on January 27, 1973 (on that side of the International Date Line). The 10 days before this date and the week after were the worst times I spent in Vietnam. The agreement basically allowed that whomever had a flag flying over their village on that day agreed that a certain four-country force could come in and assume ownership of that village. So there was massive land-grabbing going on just before and just after the treaty date. On the morning of January 27, 1973, I was called by the Province Senior Advisor and told to head back to Nha Trang, as the war was over for Americans in the field.

I had spent the previous days at our district in Dien Kanh, and when I got this call over the radio, we were pinned down under a bridge less than two kilometers from the district compound while heading for Nha Trang. The word had obviously not gotten out. It would be another eight hours before we made it to Nha Trang and only then via helicopter. Before I left country on February 21, the world had changed. We were now living in Nha Trang and I was able to interact with the Province Commander (Colonel Priat who had been with the French at Dien Bien Phu) and his deputy, Lieutenant Colonel Trac, a Dalat Military Academy graduate. It was during this time that another facet of this war was driven home to me.

By now, MACV Team 46 was shrinking fast. There were still three FSOs from the Department of State and I was the last MilOps member of MACV Team 46. I witnessed Col. Priat releasing all prisoners within his province. They were provided with orange pajamas, for lack of a better description, and set free. This almost killed him. Before I left a few days later, I rounded up all excess military equipment left within MACV Team 46 that was not carried on any property book (we had lots of stuff not on the property books that had been acquired over the years) and turned this over to Col. Priat and Lt. Col. Trac the day I left for Saigon to head back to the US. When I gave this to them, I could see the fear in their eyes. It was dawning on them that we were leaving, abandoning them. This became more evident in the months to come, but they could sense it in February of 1973. I did not fully process this at the time, as I was overcome with my own visions of going back to the US after one year and three days in Vietnam. This, after having been told I probably would not make it there from the beginning.

On February 21, 1973, my freedom bird lifted off from Ton Son Nhut and headed to Hawaii. About an hour into this flight, we were told that we were being rerouted to Kadena, Okinawa, as we were slated to land at Travis at about the same time as returning POWs of our own. They did not want us confusing the press or interfering with reunions, so to Okinawa we went. We were on the ground there for about five hours and, during this time, we headed to the officers' club and I got about as drunk as I have ever been, but that is probably because I never drank much. I do not remember any of the trip from Kadena to Travis, but we arrived at about 7:00 a.m.

For some reason unknown to me, they parked the plane about a mile from the small terminal and we deplaned and walked. We could see the empty viewing stands and press areas, but we were not returning heroes; just some soldiers who had spent a year trying to do our jobs and live to tell about it. We processed through customs and were shuttled out the door. I remember standing there thinking *What the hell is going on?* After several minutes it became obvious there was to be no one with information about transportation nor buses to the airport in San Francisco. Several others and I decided to call for a limo to take us the airport and it arrived about in an hour and a half after the call.

It was all very perplexing. I do not know what I expected, but it wasn't what was taking place. Once in the airport, we all went to the USO and "rented" a shower and changed into greens, went to book flights and spend part of the wait eating the first good meal any of us had in a long while. My flight was not slated to leave until about 8:30 p.m., headed from San Francisco to Atlanta, where I would pick up a flight to North Carolina. I arrived in my home at about 11:00 a.m. to 13 inches of snow. This was the most snow in southeastern North Carolina on record. But I was home.

It has now been 31 years since I left Vietnam, and I have still not figured out what this experience was all about. I may never figure it all out. Maybe that is the way it is with all wars and all the veterans of such. I do know that I am richer for the experience and have an understanding of things inexplicable to those who have not taken that route.

I do not have a single 'Nam veteran friend or acquaintance, male or female, who has not been divorced. Not one. I don't know what that means, maybe nothing, but that stat is significantly higher than that of our parents' generation.

Bob Flournoy

BOB FLOURNOY

I am dead at 19.
The souls of my unborn children strain at the boundaries of the universe screaming for release,
demanding their days in the sun.
They are pursued by the progeny of dead generations lurking in the shadows and swallowed
by the black hole of my early death,
Never to witness the star fire and comet glitz
Of their own passing.
Their light will never shine.
I am dead
And so are they.
Did they see me?
Did anyone?

Bob Flournoy, 1972

Charlie Two Step

Bob Flournoy

We were out a couple of days up north of Xuan Loc and the platoon I was walking with had to cross a significant blue. Anything designated as a creek or stream on those old French maps we had was shown as a blue line, so, they were blues. Crossing them always carried a degree of risk, because men were exposed and vulnerable. Standard SOP was to get the M60 across the stream first, and set it up to cover the rest of the group as they came across one at a time, at staggered intervals. Anyway, the current of this blue had washed away at the base of a tree on the edge of the stream bed for long enough to expose the roots, which hung out over the edge of the far bank, into the water. The men were using its roots to pull themselves up onto the far side.

One of the guys, a big fellow from Nebraska, let out a yelp and snatched his hand back when he reached in to grab a root, and a little green bamboo viper was thrashing around on the end of his arm. Its little fangs had embedded themselves into this guy's knuckle. These vipers were called Mr. Two Step, because that is reputedly how many steps you took after being bitten before you died. After slinging the snake downstream, this man and the rest of the unit made it across without further incident and formed a defensive perimeter deeper into the bush to see what kind of care the snake bite victim might need.

He said he felt okay, since the snake's fangs had hit bone and that had kept the venom from being pumped into his flesh. We moved out and found a night defensive position to set up in. Just after dark, the kid who had been bitten started getting very sick and started going into shock. The poison had finally done its work. Now it was dark, we were deep into Indian country, and no suitable LZ showed anywhere on our maps so that we could get a chopper in to extract him. We were in triple canopy, so we could not JP him out, so we had to ruck up and move two klicks in pitch black jungle to find an area that a medivac bird could maneuver into. We had no idea where Charlie was, but we figured he now knew where we were.

Spiders as big as your face spun webs between trees in those jungles, hoping to catch parakeets, so when a web hit our faces in that blackness, we knew that Mr. Spider was sitting a few inches away; hard not to moan, whimper or something. We finally got to an area of light growth and a medivac bird came upon frequently and told us to have our boy ready, because he did not want to hover very long, exposed to the surrounding country. He would have, mind you, but he'd rather not. I asked for illumination rounds to be shot in such a way that they would drift over the pick up zone and show the pilot where to come down. I got a negative from higher up because the ash and trash of the illumes had plotted to drift down into a no-fire zone.

Our boy was dying and I told the CO of the Divarty FDC who was giving me grief that I would kick his ass, regardless of his rank, as soon as I got out of the bush if he did not fire our illumes. The company commander told him that he would shoot him. Still no-go as the politics of no-fire zones were dictating the moment. We wasted a lot of time before somebody with balls enough back at HQ gave the go-ahead to illuminate the area. This kind of ass-covering had become commonplace late in the war, with politics calling the shots, and it cost a lot of American lives. I have no idea what happened to the kid we were trying to medivac. He never rejoined the unit.

Rob Stewart, Fred Vengelen, Bob Flournoy 1971

The Tyranny of Conformity Starts Early

Ray Hill

When I was in the first grade, my father was posted to Thailand for an 18-month assignment. My mother, brother, sister and I moved to Augusta, Georgia, to spend the 18 months living with my grandparents. We moved in the spring of that year, and I went from a school in Chicago to William Robinson Elementary in Augusta for the last few months of first grade. We had only been in Chicago about nine months and had been in Kansas for one year before that, so moving was not a traumatic event for me. On the contrary, I was excited to be living with my grandparents and in their big, old (built around 1850) house.

The school was less than a ten-minute walk from my grandparents' house and I settled immediately and comfortably into Miss Sharon's class. In Chicago, the school day had ended early and I had gone home for lunch. At William Robinson, we had lunch at school, a new and exciting activity for me. There was a lunch room in the school, but no cafeteria, so we all brought our lunches from home. In Miss Sharon's first grade class, we assembled by lining up against the wall before marching single-file into the lunch room.

One day, not long after arriving in Augusta, I took my place in line next to a girl I did not know yet. She turned to me and spoke with a wonderful Georgian accent. Her's was not the twangy, caricatured Southern accent you hear on television or from Hollywood. Her words were soft and slow and perfectly articulated—which made their affect all the worse for me. What she said in that soft voice was, "Don't you know you aren't supposed to bring your lunch in a *town* bag? You are supposed to bring your lunch in a *grocery* bag."

At first I was mystified. What could she possibly mean? Then I looked down the row of school children: all were carrying the brown bags their mothers had saved from trips to the grocery store (pre-packaged bags did not exist then—and would have been considered a silly extravagance anyway). All, that is, except me. My lunch was in a *green* bag from Belks, the big down-town department store. I was speechless in my mortification. I mumbled something like "Oh!" and then marched to lunch, hanging my head. I hoped that not too many others in my class would notice my "town" bag, which went into the trash at the earliest possible moment.

That afternoon, as soon as I had walked home from school, I went straight to my mother and asked how she could possibly have put me in such an embarrassing position. After all, she was from Augusta. Didn't she know the customs here? My mother's response was perfect. Once she understood what I was talking about—which probably wasn't easy—she assured me that I would never have to take my lunch in a town bag again. She didn't try to point out the ridiculousness of the situation. That would never have worked, with the shame of the incident so fresh in my mind.

At First There Was Wiffle Ball

Ray Hill

In the fall of 1956, I was nine years old and my brother was seven. We lived in a Virginian suburb of Washington, D.C. At that point in our lives, baseball was just a game we played with each other and friends in the neighborhood. We hadn't ever seen a real game (a year later, our father would begin taking us to Griffith stadium to watch the Senators flop around at the bottom of the American League). It was still two years before we would play organized baseball.

Like any brothers that close in age, we competed in everything: marbles, basketball, throwing stones at each other's toy soldiers in staged battles. Since my younger brother was a precocious athlete, our rivalries were even closer than usual for brothers two years apart. One day that fall, my brother reported hearing about the existence of the "World Series," in which two teams called the "Yankees" and the "Dodgers" were playing. In an instant, we had lined up on opposite sides: he chose the Dodgers and I, the Yankees; although we didn't know a player on either team and certainly didn't know the difference between Brooklyn and the Bronx. From that ignorant beginning, we would root faithfully for these teams well into our adult years. We were Army brats and our stay in Virginia lasted only a few more years. We would move four times between that fall and the end of high school. Getting started in a new place was never difficult for us. Sports were our universal medium to enter a new community. Besides, we always had each other as companions, so I never remember any moments of loneliness. Playing wiffle ball was one of the ways we kept ourselves busy when it was just the two of us. Wiffle ball was a game made to order for two players. In fact, the way we played it, any other players would have been a distraction. We played according to (what I suppose are) the normal rules. There was no base running. Hits were determined by knocking the ball past marked-off distances (e.g., a bush, a tree or a sidewalk). Outs were strike-outs, pop-ups or intercepting ground balls before they reached the distance marker for a single. Beyond these simple rules, however, we personalized the game by stepping into the roles of "our" teams and the individual players on those teams.

In our one-on-one games, my brother was the Dodgers; I was the Yankees. We followed the line-up closely. Since we are both right-handers, I couldn't choose to be Whitey Ford as a pitcher and my brother couldn't be Sandy Koufax. That still left Drysdale, Sherry, Turley and Larson to imitate. Although we could only throw right-handed, we hit from both sides of the plate. I was a righty when Bobby Richardson's turn came in the line-up and a lefty for Yogi Berra. When switch hitter Mickey Mantle was up, I learned that I could hit for power from the left but average from the right. In the same way my brother went to bat on the right side for Tommy Davis, the left for Duke Snyder and had his choice when it was Jim Gilliam's turn. I remember the agony I felt when Mantle, my ultimate hero, had a poor game. It was of very little consolation that, say, Clete Boyer had gone five for five in the same game.

The game was always fluid, since no plastic ball stayed intact very long when constantly hit by an wooden bat (metal bats were still years away). Although my children have buckets of baseballs at home, in that more frugal age we were usually working with a single ball. When it began to fall apart, we would begin a constant cycle of taping and re-taping it. With every new taping would come new aerodynamics.

"JUST A LITTLE RAIN..."

An unadulterated wiffle ball is difficult to throw with any speed and tends to curve uncontrollably. A wiffle ball bound by a layer of electrical tape moves fast and allows even unskilled arms to throw an array of pitches: sliders, curves and an occasional knuckleball in honor of Hoyt Wilhelm (even though he was an Oriole). I don't have any clear memory of a game ending because we had enough of it. What sticks in my head are games ended by darkness, my mother's call to dinner or, tragically, a ball so destroyed that no amount of tape would hold it together.

The Wall

Bob Flournoy

The second time I went to the Vietnam Memorial was more meaningful than the first. That initial time in 1982 was a circus. Absolute carnival atmosphere that agitated, angered me. Balloons, snacks, crowds, an absolute lack of the sober, subdued, holy atmosphere that I expected and that, in my mind, the shrine demanded. The place was still relatively new, and it was a summer Saturday with the sun shining, which encouraged the throngs to turn out, which included, unfortunately, a couple hundred guys who thought that they needed to dress up like bikers in old fatigues which were plastered with ribbons and patches, boonie hats and the obligatory granny shades. And head bands. And drooping mustaches. All carrying on with one another, hugging, power handshaking, crocodile tears, milling around on the path directly in front of the black depths of that wall, here I am check me out. Dude. Total bullshit. I have found that for every ten guys who tell you they were in 'Nam, as many as half are lying, and when it comes to who did what, most of them were airborne ranger CIB gun-slinging bad asses who stalked the jungle with cold steel resolve and by God I've earned my booze but don't talk to me too much about it because once established that I am the real deal then we just don't go there. Man. Total bullshit.

Second trip was also a Saturday, many years later, in the fall, nippy with some bluster in the wind, fading color in the hardwoods. Only a couple dozen older people paused reflectively in front of the mirrored finish of names, some hesitantly rubbing names off onto various finishes and fabrics, almost apologetically, standing silently looking down at their work to see if some magic would appear, some who looked at the name they had sought out with a sense of bewilderment, trying to comprehend after 30 years or more. A few guys my age in jeans, sweatshirts, light jackets, graying, thinning hair, standing off a little with arms crossed, unmoving, looking for something that they were not having any luck finding: quiet, pensive, detached.

    I stood awhile, also detached, eyes glazing off into the distant depths of the marble, wandered off, found a to-go coffee and drifted back onto the grass to resume watch for awhile longer. I didn't seek out the names this time. I knew where they were. Still.

The Real Fun Begins

Ray Hill

In 1961, a time of great Cold War tension, I had the opportunity to go to Berlin, Germany. It was just a few days before the Wall went up, dividing the city for the next thirty years. But my visit to Berlin was completely unconnected to geo-politics. I was there for a baseball tournament: the Babe Ruth League (ages 13 to 15) championship of Germany. The tournament started in the first week of August and, due to rain interruptions, spilled over into the second week. My memories of that visit to Berlin have a surreal quality: fun and games, preceded by just a few days, the awful event of Sunday, August 13.

As you might suspect, the contenders for the Babe Ruth championship of Germany were not German boys, but rather teams from US Army and Air Force bases. (At the next level, the European championships, non-American teams actually participated, but in a special bracket. Those teams of European nationals weren't very good, but we Americans were amazed that *any* teenagers in, say, Holland, were playing baseball—where did they find a field to play on in a country of rectangular soccer fields?)

I played for the "Main Valley All-stars," chosen from the Army posts where the Third Infantry Division was located. One of the great things about our league was that we had to travel for each game—through unbelievably beautiful German countryside that probably hadn't changed much in appearances from medieval times—castles on the hills, wagons in the fields still drawn by horses. When the regular season ended, the "All Stars" were gathered in Wurzburg, the home of the league champion, for a couple of days of practice before the trip to Berlin.

The train ride to Berlin was the only time during the whole trip when we had any sense of the Cold War menace that weighed down on the city. The ride was a long one since, from Wurzburg, we had to travel initially in a northwesterly direction, away from Berlin to connect with the corridor where trains from the west were allowed to approach Berlin. Most of the trip was at night, and any stop along the way had us fourteen- and fifteen-year-olds worried about what might happen in "enemy" territory. We all knew why our fathers were here in Germany.

Once we arrived in Berlin, however, we were in familiar territory. For boys of that age, the tournament was a terrific lark. The only adults with us were three coaches who kept only a loose watch. When we weren't playing baseball we were on our own, far away from restraining parents. Since the tournament was interrupted by several days of rain we had a lot of time on our own. We didn't actually behave much differently than had we been at home—we went to the movies, played basketball in the post gym and hung out at the snackbar. It was just the idea of independence that was so exhilarating. Even the one trip we took into the Eastern Zone was empty of Cold War nuance. We visited the vast Russian cemetery and memorial to the Soviet soldiers killed in the Second World War. Our trip there was mostly through the showcase streets in the East, lined with modern office and apartment buildings. I can only remember a brief glimpse at the shoddy buildings and sites still unreconstructed from the war, which filled most of East Berlin outside the showcase zone. Passage into the Eastern Zone was completely routine, even so close to the creation of the Wall.

The weather was cool and rainy, which gave rise to the highlight of the tournament. We kids didn't care how long we were footloose in Berlin, but I'm sure the adults were beginning to worry about how long the tournament would take, because steady rain kept leading to postponements. One afternoon, the rain stopped and the coaches assessed the playing conditions on the field. A short time later, two helicopters appeared to "blow dry" the outfield—one advantage of playing on an Army post. They hovered a few feet in the air as all of us cheered. I'm not sure the helicopters accomplished much, but they certainly entertained us.

I never did see the Wall. It went up on the weekend and we departed in the middle of the week. By the time I visited Berlin again in the 1990s, the Wall was gone. Berlin is a beautiful city now, but I saw no evidence of that baseball tournament. When the city's current residents asked me the occasion for my previous visit, it took some time to convince them I wasn't crazy.

Never Enough Games

Ray Hill

When those of us who are middle-aged (and beyond) reminisce about our youthful baseball, we tend to recollect the unsupervised games at our local playgrounds. There were no coaches or parents, nor did anyone schedule these games. Maybe we grabbed some other kids on our block, but mostly we went out to the playground at times we thought the other neighborhood kids might be hanging out with a glove and bat and a ball. All of us seem to regret the fact that our children seem to play baseball in a much more organized form. Well, as much as I enjoyed those pick-up games, I do have a conflicting emotion. I remember just how wonderful it was to look forward to a *game*—I mean a real game, with coaches, umpires and uniforms. A game was special and formal and, therefore, the experience richer and sweeter.

A real game meant that we had the right equipment. At least at the start of play we had a spotless white baseball. We also had catcher's equipment, which was almost never present at a pick-up game. Catcher's equipment made it easier for the pitcher to throw better pitches. It also meant that someone could catch the ball and throw it promptly back to the pitcher. In pick-up ball, to avoid having a foul ball take your teeth out, we usually chased down a missed pitch after it hit the backstop. The whole rhythm and sound of the game picked up. You need to have a catcher to hear the "whap" of a fast pitch that sounds so satisfying to the pitcher and so terrifying to the batter.

A real game upped the ante for performance. We were playing in front of our coach. An objective umpire called the balls and strikes—no arguing or whining to change a call. Someone was actually recording in the scorebook whether we hit or struck-out. Most often, the players on the other team were strangers to us—menacing strangers at the beginning of a game. Somehow, it meant more to succeed or fail in front of anonymous observers than in front of familiar friends. How hard could they hit the ball? What kind of stuff would the pitcher have? We would have no idea until the game started. I don't remember ever starting a game without butterflies in my stomach.

A real game usually meant we were playing on a field with a fence, dugouts (even if they were usually entirely above ground) and, maybe, a reasonable amount of grass. The pick-up games were mostly in an open field. With a fence, it was possible to hit a "real" home run. The bases were square, made of canvas and the right distance from each other, not four rocks or pieces of cardboard at an approximation of right angles. The foul lines were limed—again, no arguing over fair and foul.

Finally, a real game meant uniforms. Baseball uniforms are so much *unlike* normal clothes that just to put on a uniform has a transforming affect. Putting on a baseball uniform emphasizes purpose and commitment. The uniforms of forty and fifty years ago enhanced that emphasis. The cloth was thick flannel—why would anyone wear flannel on a hot summer day unless he were dead serious about the purpose of the activity? We usually didn't own the uniforms. In that age of non-disposability, they were the property of the team and handed over from one year's boys to the next. To be allowed to wear such a timeless community property was thrilling. We did own our hats, and these were precious. They were not the adjustable hats of today, and we didn't have a closet full of hats with dozens of different logos on them.

It may seem perverse, but games were so much fun precisely because they *were* so formal, because everything counted more than in pick-up. The uniforms, coaches and umpires all meant that the enterprise was worth your whole effort and imagination. It was the only occasion I can remember when adults were investing a great deal of time with no purpose other than to provide an environment where we could play. (In Scouts and Sunday School, the adults were also out to teach us something.) We looked (or thought we looked) like major leaguers. I sure that feeling made us want to play better.

What keeps the memory of these games so precious in my mind was that there were so few of them. My son, who plays in the league at his neighborhood park, may play dozens games each spring and summer—and he could elect to play another ten or so in the fall. And he has been doing so since we was a tee-baller at the age of five. I didn't start organized sports of any kind until I was eleven (probably typical for my generation) and a normal season may have been a dozen games at most. (My junior varsity team in high school in Carlisle, Pennsylvania, played only seven games in the spring of 1963!) I will go to my grave with a hunger to play one more *real* baseball game.

You Never Remember the Details

Bob Flournoy

It must have been easier in WWII and Korea to remember the particulars of events that could be described as "combat." With some exceptions, of course, whole divisions, armies even, were on line with clear-cut objectives, knowing where the enemy was and where your own guys were. That certainly didn't make it any easier, but it did add some definition to the confusion of battle and made remembering how situations unfolded years later a little easier. In 'Nam, small groups of kids in the dark jungle whose boredom and the drudgery of moving through the bush, interrupted with a rush of unexpected violence ending as quickly as it began, makes for hazy memories. The sudden, brief violence of these typical encounters left only a colorful blur as a memory in most cases. I wouldn't give too much credence to anyone who tells you a detailed account of a particular conflict in the bush in 'Nam. Actually, I believe very few people when they tell me a war story in great detail. It was a long time ago, and the mind tends to go numb in those situations of great stress, noise and confusion, where all mental facilities are overloaded simultaneously. Firefights in the dark of the jungle are like one big stun grenade. No one is immune and the details become a blur, even seconds after the encounter is over. But, okay, there was this one time that I remember…

"JUST A LITTLE RAIN..."

After moving all day long in dead quiet, single file, through some very thick triple-canopy jungle, numb with the heat, humidity, hunger, thirst and bone-dead fatigue of it all, the world exploded at the head of the column when the point man let go with his buckshot loaded shotgun, his pace man ripped off a whole magazine from his M-16 on full automatic, and, a split second later, the rest of the platoon, instantly prone on the ground, fired everything they had into the dark around them for a very noisy mad minute of tracers that chewed into the dark in an absolutely deafening roar, until the word came back down the line that the point man had looked up into the face of a 20-foot python that was hanging down from the tree an inch in front of his face, evoking the shotgun response point blank into that poor snake's head, and of course setting off the chain reaction that followed. We had to get that kid some clean britches, even though he had only worn his for two weeks. The CO was furious because we had announced to anyone within six grid squares that we were there, although they probably thought we were a reinforced battalion from the ruckus we kicked up.

I was halfway through my tour, even though, as Yogi Berra used to say, the second half is 90% of it.

Germany, 1960s

Ed Condon

At 48 years of age, I continue to be stumped by the question, "So, where are you from?" Well let's see, I was born in Detroit but we moved when I was four, so I'm really not "from" there. I've lived in two countries, seven states and attended more primary and secondary schools than I can remember. The only way I can really answer that question is, "I was an Army brat." Not sure where that expression comes from or exactly what it means. To me, it used to mean that I was cheated out of the consistency of growing up with the same friends, attending the same schools and developing lifelong relationships. Nowadays, I have learned that almost everyone I know who grew up that way has long since lost contact with those so-called lifelong friends. I didn't have the chance to develop long-term friendships, but I never lacked for friends. When my dad would get transferred to a new assignment, I'd find the closest playground or ball field and hang out. It wasn't long before a game of something started. In the summer it was usually baseball, or we played "army." In the winter it was snowball fights, sledding, war, or a combination of the three. All boys like to play war. I guess we were following in our fathers footsteps.

Growing up on an Army post was like growing up in Mayberry. You could leave the house in the morning, play all day, eat lunch at a friend's house and return for dinner without any questions. I never remember hearing about anything bad happening to a kid. These long days of innocence and freedom frequently resulted in the ritual summer sandlot baseball games. I would learn later in life that most of my friendships would be centered around sports. I think every boy played baseball, so you immediately had something in common with the other boys. Choices of summer activities for kids were limited. You could read or play baseball. I didn't know any boys who read during the day. New kids were always moving in, others were transferred out. I had a lot of best friends who moved. We'd always promise to write and sometimes shared a letter or two, but it never lasted. I think growing up in a military family prepares you for life. For the most part, being an adult is a lot like growing up in a military family. People move a lot, friendships are mostly transient, and change is constant. Some things should never change; that's why I don't like the designated-hitter rule.

My oldest memory of baseball is somewhat blurred because I was so young. My dad took me to a Detroit Tiger's game when I was a four years old. I don't really remember the game that much, but it was exciting and the hot dogs were good. My dad really liked baseball; especially his beloved Tigers. Sometime that same year, my father was transferred to Germany. This was the early 60s, but technologically we stepped back in time about a decade. There was no television and only one radio station, but lots of baseball. We never really had to organize a game. One kid, bat and glove over shoulder, would walk down the street toward the sand lot. He was like the pied-piper. Boys would grab their gloves and walk with a sense of expectation and urgency to the makeshift diamond. We were basically poor, but didn't know it. All we needed was one bat, one ball and enough gloves to equip one team in the field. To this day, I can remember the ritual of throwing (you never handed) your glove to another kid as your team headed in to take turns at bat. Through the construction of the Berlin Wall, the Cuban Missile Crisis and the potential threat of the Russian invasion, we played baseball. We were oblivious to everything going on around us—we were Mickey Mantle, Roger Maris and Ted Williams. Our world was an innocent place where the rules were clear and the stakes were neighborhood bragging rights. We played until it was dark or someone's Mom called the first kid in for dinner. The next day, the process repeated. The pied-piper walked down the street and, the next thing you knew, it was dinner time.

As one of them dwarves in Lord of the Rings *said after that really big fight with the goblins and orcs, "We all do one thing in our lives in which our hearts forever dwell." That thing, unfortunately, is often war. But, just because you didn't have cause to go through it doesn't mean you would not have done just fine. It is in us to be as good as we have to be, especially when others are counting on us, and when the stakes are life and death, there is no room for error, and you almost never get a second chance.*

First Blush

Bob Flournoy, III

When we reported for Officer Basic Course in the spring of 1970, we were an odd assortment of ROTC graduates, West Point graduates and National Guardsmen newly commissioned through their state programs. Desperate for officers in that year, we also had among us some direct-commissioned warrant officers who had served tours in 'Nam and had accepted the Army's offer to become officers and gentlemen. These guys were inevitably helicopter pilots who now needed their branch-specific training; in this case, field artillery. We were there to learn the complicated science of projectile ballistics, survey, precise map-reading, fire direction computing, fire adjustment from the ground, and from the air. Curiously, we never had any instruction on how to bring fire in close by ear, and that is exactly how we would all be doing it in the very near future, in jungle so thick that you could barely see the sky.

You are never without a unit designation in the Army. The minute you leave one unit on orders for another, you are part of that new home. So it was that we were members of a school battalion at Ft. Sill, Oklahoma, and that is where we reported prior to our branch training. We had the obligatory formation so that the company commander of the "school company" could give us a once over and make sure that we knew how to put our brass on and straighten our gig lines. West Pointers and ROTC guys got a nod and glare from the little peacock school CO who had never been out of that garrison in his entire short career, but the law school graduates who had been assigned to a combat arms officer basic training outfit were a little rusty, with green brass and Hershey bar shoes. The little peacock admonished them in that first formation as they sullenly stared over his head, but he was at a loss for words when he stood in front of the seasoned ex-warrant officers who had a fistful of Distinguished Flying Crosses and Silver Stars on their chests, the results of many tours in 'Nam flying gun ships. He stopped in front of an old-salt warrant standing next to me who had more color on his chest than a baboon's ass, and, at a loss for words, he poked him in his generous stomach and told him that he might try a little PT. My new hero looked him right in the eye and said, "Why don't you go fuck yourself?" Captain Peacock, white as a sheet, turned around and walked into his office and we never saw him again.

    I don't believe this old gunship pilot, now a new officer and gentleman, ever had to buy a beer for the rest of the course.

Lockport, New York

Mike Marotta

Now that I'm an adult, I realize how unique my childhood really was. Back then, I thought everyone lived next door to their aunts and uncles and that life was all about baseball in the backyard in the summer, and freezing the ball field for pick-up hockey in the winters. It's funny how the past doesn't really change, but your perspectives on the past are shaped by present-day events.

I came from a broken family at a time when divorce wasn't quite so common. The thing was, it was common to me; I was four years old, so I don't really remember much more than, "Dad lives somewhere else and I sleep there sometimes." We lived with my grandmother in the house her husband built. I say "her husband," because my grandfather died two years before I was born. I've seen pictures… he looked liked someone I would've wanted to know.

My grandfather was apparently quite a guy, because he bought all the neighboring lots and gave them to my grandmother's brothers and sisters as wedding gifts. So there we were, one family in four straight houses on the outskirts of the town of Lockport, New York—home of the Erie Canal's famous locks, the world's widest bridge, Reid's Drive-In (where you can still bring a date and eat lunch for about five bucks), and about the only thing wedged between Buffalo and Canada.

I was the youngest kid around and my mom had to work, so I spent a lot of time with my grandmother. We watched *Sesame Street*, *The*

"JUST A LITTLE RAIN..."

Electric Company, *Romper Room*, and *The Uncle Bobby Show* together (the latter, on Canada's CFTO Channel 9, was a local favorite that I now look back on as a freakish old dude who's more than a little scary). I can still hear her drilling me about the letters and numbers, and I just couldn't seem to learn enough from her. She was, and is, all about saving things and doing the most with the least... and she had the coolest stuff of anyone I know. Having grown up during the Depression, she saved absolutely everything—she even washed and re-used paper plates.

I learned more during those days, I think, than I learned in my first few years of school. In fact, it was my grandmother who first taught me how to play baseball. She was home and I wanted to learn to play, so we went in the backyard with a ball and played catch. Every day, we would go out and practice. It confounded the neighbors a bit, who were all right-handed, because my grandmother is a lefty. So, naturally, she taught me how to play left-handed. As a result, I never had to worry about hand-me-down gloves. I still look back on those days and picture myself as a kid in the backyard, tossing the ball around with a 60-year-old woman in a housecoat and a hairnet. Even with that uniform, she was still pretty damn good.

We all played baseball back then—moms, aunts, uncles, cousins, and siblings. My uncles built a backstop in the back corner of our yard, and our home field was the site for some spirited family entertainment. I can still remember the summer we cleared the area for what would be our ball field. There were about ten of us with our generation's weed whackers—scythes—chopping away at the weeds, fending off field mice, mosquitoes, ticks, and local snakes (which got pretty large, even though they were harmless). Most people think it can't get that hot in Lockport, NY, but let me tell you, that summer it felt like we were working on the surface of the sun. We couldn't wait for the occasional lemonade and "off" break, and the end-of-day trip to Aunt Eva & Uncle Barty's house (two doors down), where our family pool was situated.

There was always pop in Aunt Eva's downstairs fridge (that's soda, or coke, for those people challenged by the Western NY terminology), and Hershey's miniatures in the candy dish. There were all sorts of other treasures in Aunt Eva's house, too. I can remember vividly, taking the walk through the 70s beads (like Greg had on *The Brady Bunch*) into the little bathroom. There were all sorts of funny little off-color trinkets, and a sign with some sage advice:

If you sprinkle when you tinkle, be a sweetie, wipe the seatie.

I've never seen that sign anywhere else, so I'm thinking maybe my aunt wrote it herself. She and my Uncle Barty were about the best people I've ever met. Aunt Eva was not quite five feet tall, even with the beehive, but she was an absolute spitfire. She had a wonderful sense of humor and a great singing voice, but as long as she lived I never once saw her go in that swimming pool. Everyone always said she didn't want to get her hair wet, but I always wondered if there wasn't something more to it.

Uncle Barty was originally from Canada and had lost a piece of one finger in World War II. He was always in the yard, trimming a tree or cutting the grass. It seemed like he cut that grass every day. When he wasn't working the yard, he was cleaning the pool, trying to keep it spotless for us and all of our friends. If there were enough of us there, he'd show up with a pocket full of coins and start throwing them in the water. I'm not sure why, but we just loved diving for change. He was my surrogate father growing up, the "man" I looked to for advice and as a role model for right and wrong. The day he died is still the worst day of my life. Maybe it was the Canada thing that fueled our love for the game, and I know it contributed to the various home rinks we had over the years.

That all started one late fall day, when we (the kids) decided on our own that if we shoveled the snow out to form a rectangle and then flooded Uncle Phil's front yard, we could make our own hockey rink. It was a pretty ambitious project, since the oldest among us in this conspiracy, my cousin Chris, was about 12 years old. As sure as Buffalo winters are cold, our efforts paid off, and we had a little rink to play on. I was most often the goalie during that first winter. I was five years old and hadn't yet learned to skate, so I taped some foam rubber to my legs, and with a hockey glove and stick in one hand and a metal garbage can lid in the other, I defended the area between the two empty crates that served as a net.

My cousin Mike, who is about ten months older than I am, taught me how to skate and play hockey that winter: no small feat for a six-year-old. He had started playing on a team, which made me long for "real hockey," too. When I started playing a year later, we decided we would both go pro and play for the Sabres. Ah, the dreams of youth.

Over the years, our ambitions and home rinks grew together. By the time we were in high school, we had a real rink about half the size of a pro arena behind my Uncle Cam's house. The uncles had pitched in and rented a backhoe, and they dug out the area. We all had fun that first fall, barefoot and knee-deep in water, pulling every plant out at the roots to make sure we would have a smooth surface when it froze. My uncles and older cousins ran electricity and hung lights at either end of the rink, and they built a small shack so we wouldn't have to trek back to and from the ice on skates. Our nets were fashioned out of steel piping and chain link fence, and we spray-painted the pucks a bright orange so we could find them easier in the dark. That rink was a sanctuary all through my young life. Even after we moved out of Gram's house and into our own, I would go there to skate. I'd stop in to see Gram, have some hot chocolate with her, and spend hours at a time working on skating, stick-handling, and shooting. The one-on-one games were oftentimes the most fun, matching skills with Mike, who I've never quite been able to beat. I am an inch or two taller than he is, though, so I guess that counts for something!

Mike was always one age group above me, so we never really played together until high school. I remember how proud Uncle Barty was to finally see us on the ice for the same team. It was my freshman year and Mike's sophomore season. We didn't play on the same line, since we were both centers, but we did get to skate together on special teams. Uncle Barty was always there, and I can still see him in the same spot, behind the goal at the old Kenan Center, watching through the scratched-up Plexiglas. He was there for about a month of the season, and then, in an instant, everything changed. On October 26 of that year, he got up from the dinner table, clutched his chest, and then fell to the floor. I wanted so desperately to make the big time, to make him proud just one more time, but it wasn't to be. I was never quite good enough, and Mike and I together are about big enough to make one NHL player. I realized though, that I could honor his memory in other ways.

It's been about the joy of the game for a long time. I'm not as young as I once was, but I still play hockey. I see a lot of my uncle in Wayne, the guy who runs our men's league team; I guess that's why we get along so well. I also coach, one of the great joys in my life, and I think about Uncle Barty every time I step on the ice.

Those years on Chestnut Ridge Road have really left their mark on my life. Gram turned 90 this year, and I recently found out that she's selling her house; a house she's lived in for over 60 years... my home for my first 10 years. It's sad to think about someone else living there, but I guess all things must change.

I have an old medal of my uncle's. It's been in my wallet since the day he died; every day but one. On that day, September 4, 1993, I held it tightly in my hand at the altar of a church in Lockport, NY, as I made my wedding vows to the love of my life.

My son, Jake, bears Uncle Barty's name in the middle, and every once in a while, I see the same twinkle in Jake's eye as I used to see in Uncle Barty's—that little bit of mischief under the surface, and I know he's there, watching and protecting. My daughter, Emily, was born on April 9, a day after Gram's birthday. We tried very hard to have them share a birthday. Expecting that Jenni would need a C-section as she had with Jake, we scheduled it for April 8. But Emily would have none of it—she wanted her own day. So much like Aunt Eva... so much like Gram.

The past was a long time ago...but, then again, maybe it really isn't so far away. I can go there anytime I feel like it.

Mike Marotta

The Rest of Hopke's Story

John R. Hopke, Jr.

My father was not in combat during his Persian Gulf command-stationing late in World War II nor during his term in Korea. He'd been out of the service for a while between those conflicts, but joined back up when carrying an insurance book around the streets of Brooklyn, along with civilian life in general, didn't seem to work out. While I was growing up, he seemed to me to be an anomaly. Whenever he was in the US, he managed to arrange assignments to the New York metropolitan area, so the family maintained a home outside the city, and he lived the life of a commuter.

I don't think my friends quite understood how he could be in the Army and do that, nor how he could be gone for years at a time. In the same fashion in which I had acknowledged him by taking his confirmation name as my own five years earlier, I applied for ROTC membership prior to departing for college, despite sensing, to the degree that I knew myself at all, that I simply wasn't suited for it.

(I want to say that I wrote much of the earlier personal information in this piece to try to establish a basis for what I hope can be seen as a continuity in my actions from then to the following. It must be seen that I did not respect my father. My father was to me then an alcoholic, and an embarrassment.)

My father arranged for my qualifying physical to take place at the reserve center in Lower Manhattan, where he worked. In the presence of his superior officers and fellow NCOs, he and I were informed that I failed. The teeth which Army dentists had drilled, filled, and extracted literally dozens of times during my childhood and adolescence, and now the periodontal area, as well, were deemed to be so faulty as to constitute liabilities to myself and the service.

Here now was the break I certainly knew I needed; a break not only from the seemingly very distant possibility of going to war, but also from the fear of becoming like my father, and I was prepared to drive home unburdened and neither unhappy nor embarrassed. 4-f status based on dental factors was a technicality, as far as I was concerned, and not cause to feel unfit. Had not, admirable SATs and grades aside, my perceived potential as a distance runner been a factor in my college acceptance? The matter had not, however, been resolved.

One thing my father, as an experienced military supply operative, knew how to do was deal and ask for favors. And he knew how I'd always silently acceded to his emotional manipulation; even broad, very indirect, perhaps subconscious manipulation. This time, he approached directly and specifically, and in front of that same chain of command and group of colleagues, stated more than asked, after informing me that a special arrangement might be made, "You want to go, don't you, Jackie?" I desperately did not, but to say no would have been to disavow and invalidate my father's life, to deny him utterly, to disown him publicly.

I came, thereafter, to rationalize quite effectively and often, and, not only *not* to feel soiled and diminished by undesired actions that cannot rightly be described as decisions, but to feel quite righteous about them. When the Army and my college offered me a full ROTC scholarship prior to junior year, I accepted it despite its attendant commitments of extended service and regular Army status and despite my increasing opposition to the war, deluding myself that it was an act of generosity toward the two younger brothers who needed what limited resources the family had for schooling—-they could have taken care of themselves—and that our involvement in Vietnam would end before graduation.

"JUST A LITTLE RAIN..."

I had learned nothing from a developing awareness that I was doing things that were directly contrary to what I believed and wanted and that were generated by perverse forces. I married, without a single private social contact with another woman, the first person I had dated in high school four and a half years earlier. (President Kennedy was shot the day we were to have had our first date.) That marriage commitment, in turn, provided the rationale for not refusing the military commission which preceded the wedding by seven days, graduation from college by one, transfer to Fort Benning by a fortnight, and orders to Vietnam by a year.

After going through war and divorce—-and counseling—-myself, my bitterness toward the John R., Senior, who had also worn the uniform and been left by a wife, morphed initially into guilt and self-accusation, fueled by doubts about personal integrity and self-worth. I had come, during sophomore year at college, to believe the Vietnam War to be evil, yet, three years later, I was an Airborne- and Ranger-qualified Army captain, helping fight the devastating and ultimately futile battle for Firebase Ripcord with the 3rd Battalion/504th Infantry of the 101st Airborne Division.

I returned to the United States in August of 1970 and spent two years in an easy job at Benning. I then resigned as soon as the four years of required service ended. I found a broadcasting job with a former colleague from the college radio station we'd both managed. He gave me virtually a free hand to develop a new station his family had bought, and we made a modest financial success of the business, a creative success of a commercial medium, and stars of ourselves. Things deteriorated personally in the late '70s when the progressive approach to programming became untenable, when I came home one night after a Grateful Dead concert to an empty house and a cowardly note from my wife, and when I was introduced to the drugs that seemed to dull the survivor- and participant-guilt of Vietnam. Late in 1979, I took a job back in New York managing promotions for a major record label, a stupid move even in concept, given that I loved radio and knew that I was very good at it. A change of scene seemed in order, but instead initiated a mostly unfortunate score of years that only recently ended, and whose vicissitudes surely continued to reflect the instability, unhappiness, and self-destructive behavior of my post-Vietnam years.

It's not necessary to discuss that period now. I stopped using drugs a good number of years ago and am a bit more at ease with my Vietnam involvement. I display my Ranger tab on my car. My second ex-wife, with whom I spent fifteen years, is a good friend. I played baseball (softball) again for about ten years in the '70s and '80s, with my own station upstate and in the Arts and Entertainment League in New York. Even though we both, at different points, moved away to Los Angeles, I still reflexively go to the Dodgers' score when I pick up a newspaper. I've returned to radio after twenty-four years away, hosting classical music and news programs with an NPR affiliate in New Orleans, where I've lived for eight years. I have a few well-defined goals, one or two slightly immodest but attainable, and hope to be healthy enough for long enough to see them realized, along with some lingering debts repaid.

My father remarried. In 1976, he impregnated a woman acquaintance very much his junior who had been told she'd never be able to bear children, and who had two adopted pre-teenage daughters. My father, who'd retired from the military and was about to retire again after ten years as a maintenance foreman with the Ford Motor Company, professed to all that he loved my new stepmother and that he was happy. He wrote lists of reasons why. Whereas, in the recent past, he had spoken with anticipation about enjoying a bachelor's retirement of fishing and relaxing (and perhaps a part-time Post Office job) in a modest trailer home in Florida, he now found himself at 56 with two adolescent daughters and an epileptic infant. When his health soon began to fail rapidly, he refused to go to the hospital for treatment. It took my driving to his house in New Jersey and forcing him into a car to get him there. He returned home after examination, treatment, and rest with admonitions regarding his drinking and smoking. He did not heed them.

There are ways to kill oneself and then there are ways to kill oneself. One morning in February of 1977, not too many weeks or months after his previous hospitalization, I picked up a call on the request line during my midday air shift and heard my stepmother's shaky voice. I knew immediately that my father had died. I stayed on the air for another two and a half hours until my program ended, told my general manager what had happened, then went home to pack a bag and drive to New Jersey. When I arrived, my drugged and distraught stepmother screamed at me for taking so long to get there. My wife accompanied me for one day while I helped with arrangements, then she left to go back upstate to work, without staying for the burial. My mother did not attend. I have not since visited my father's grave.

> "The most important thing a father can do for his children is to love their mother."
>
> —-Theodore M. Hesburgh (b. 1917),
> President Emeritus of the University of Notre Dame

I was asked twice within the last seven or eight years to contribute information and photographs to writers and producers of print and broadcast journalism about the battles for Firebase Ripcord, which took place in Vietnam in the spring and summer of 1970. This campaign was the last major engagement of the war, but not much was known about it until recently. The Army and the government knew from the onset that the rationale for the Ripcord stand (essentially a delaying action) was flimsy to indefensible, and when it became a battle of huge human cost that ended in withdrawal, efforts were made to limit public awareness of its magnitude. Nothing new, as this scenario had played out many times before in the war.

The first request came from Keith Nolan, a respected military historian. He was researching what would become his book entitled *Screaming Eagles Under Siege*, a detailed, insightful, and highly recommended history of the engagements. I was quite torn about providing input. I had still not yet learned to deal maturely with my own internal conflicts about participating in the war in general and I continued to question—-unjustifiably, as I later realized—-my individual performance and bravery, decorations notwithstanding. The uncertainty, indecisiveness, and, more recently, guilt, which had allowed previous major events in my life simply to take place, as you have read, led again to inaction.

I experienced some frustration on Ripcord in the exercise of my responsibilities, including command's ignoring my daily warnings about blatant personal and unit breaches of communications security, and I was aware of the very tenuous justification of our tactical and strategic operations. I was concerned that critical input I might provide Mr. Nolan would be seen as an insult to the bravery I observed every day on the part of the soldiers with whom I served. Their courage, energy, dedication, and inventiveness were astounding. I saw what was sacrificed in an environment where the prevalent attitude toward the war and death itself was, "Don't mean nothin'." In a conflict for sheer national survival the American soldier, at least the soldier of the 101st Airborne Division (Airmobile), would be indomitable.

Ignoring the second request for information and photographs, which came from a television producer just two years ago, was a simpler matter. He was preparing a *documentary* for a series hosted by Oliver North on the Fox Network. It's an easy decision not to support the commercial broadcast efforts of a company whose constant documented distortions and falsehoods might be further exacerbated by a presenter who should probably still be in jail for treason instead of on the air.

This second request does, though, put the continuing futility of much of the international conflict in which the United States has engaged in the last half-century (my lifetime from, say, First Holy Communion on) into some focus. I've often called myself a reluctant patriot. I'm not sure why, unless it has something to do with what I'm starting to see just now for myself as part of putting this little writing together, and what I'm sure I haven't perfectly aligned to the reader—-let alone myself—-as seeming parallel, and that may be that *my* nuclear family and *my* national family are the same. And we've both come apart over that same period of time for *our* refusal to recognize that that definition, that perception, is just too narrow, whether you're an Army brat or not. What have we learned from the lies and distortions (the Tonkin Gulf Resolution, the Domino Theory, "Vietnamization") that wasted so much in Southeast Asia; or from the illicit trade, theft, and deceptions of the Iran/Contra affair; or now from the dubious scenario of Iraq harboring weapons of mass destruction and acting as the nexus of a global Islamic terrorist plot?

And if I am, or have been, in so many ways, my father's son, did he not ask himself similar questions about the conflicts of the first half of the century? Did he also internalize the international enmities we were forced to believe had to exist?

Maybe that's the question to ask the next time I visit that national cemetery on Long Island.

Confusing Times and Hard Decisions

Ray Hill

I have spent a good bit of time reconsidering the history of and my views about the war in Vietnam. In contrast, I promised myself that I would not attempt to reevaluate my personal choices related to that war. I do think about the personal process I went through to make those choices. The decisions I made thirty-five years ago were made honestly in the context of that time and cannot be redone. I believe there is some value, however, in reevaluating the context in which those decisions were made. First, some background...

My father was a career infantry officer. I lived about half my life on Army posts. I was familiar with guns from an early age, taking target practice with a 22 rifle when I was five, owning my own single-barreled 410 shotgun when I was eight. I signed up for ROTC in my freshman year in college and graduated as a lieutenant in the reserves—an honor military graduate. I did not join ROTC in anticipation of a military career. In fact, my father had cautioned me not to pursue a military life. He had done so as a way out of rural Alabama in 1939. "If you do choose the military," he told me, "join another service, not the Army. And if you do join the Army, don't sign up for the infantry." He was not at all unhappy with the choice he had made for his career, but he had other hopes for me.

"JUST A LITTLE RAIN..."

Enrolling in ROTC was just a reasonable precaution. All young men of that era were subject to the draft, once out of college. Heeding at least some of my father's advice, I wanted some control over the terms of a potential entry into the armed service. While in college, I was part of a small group active in the campus Episcopal Church. We met fairly regularly to discuss the important religious issues of life that trouble all of us, especially when we are young (e.g., Why does God allow evil people to inflict pain and suffering on innocent people?). As I look back, there was a dichotomy in my intellectual life. In a number of my college courses I was confronting authors like Sartre, Camus, and Conrad who deal with the pervasive ambiguities of life. Academically, at least, I was learning that thoughtful people can ask difficult and important questions and not expect to get good answers—or any answers at all some times. Apparently I wasn't internalizing much of this academic study, however. I approached the religious discussions with an attitude that definitive answers were available to all of life's important questions, and I could find those answers if I tried hard enough.

After graduation, I went directly to graduate school. This was not an attempt to defer or escape military service, but pursuit of my desire for a Ph.D. in economics and career in teaching. I fully expected that I would complete two years eventually. I spent the first year of graduate school at the University of California at Berkeley and a second on a fellowship studying in Geneva.

Although the war in Vietnam was a central fact of life during this period, as I look back, I am struck by how isolated I was from its reality. I didn't own a television and never watched the news accounts that, I have been told, "brought the war into our living rooms." During this time, several of my friends from high school days went to fight in Vietnam, but I did not keep in touch with most of them. Most of my college classmates, even those in ROTC, were continuing their education and I was not a close friend of anyone from college who went into the military, much less to Vietnam.

The war was a constant subject of protest at Berkeley. In the spring of 1970, the US began bombing Cambodia, which gave rise to a heightened wave of anti-war activity. Some classes were suspended and demonstrations took place, which resulted in police using tear gas to disperse the protesters. The economics department was located in a minor topographical depression, where the tear gas tended to collect. My ROTC training, thankfully, had taught me the pain and nausea of tear gas. I can remember holding my breath and sprinting to higher ground to avoid it as I went home at the end of a day at school.

None of the activity connected with protesting the war brought me into contact with anyone who had first hand experience of it, much less any critical evaluation of its significance. I was sure that it was immoral—that was obvious to everyone, except those people in Washington who were evil or stupid or both.

My next year in Geneva made the war even more remote. Virtually all of my classmates were Europeans and I don't remember ever discussing the war. But it was during that year that I determined that I had to come to some fundamental judgment, not just about the war in Vietnam, but about war in general. I want to be as clear as possible about the way I looked at the world then. I was convinced that the war was a mistake, but at that point I saw no legitimate (to me, at least) grounds for not serving in the Army to complete my obligation from ROTC. As I saw it, the war in Vietnam was forcing me to confront a bigger issue. It required me to answer for myself the question of whether war was ever moral. Up to that point in my life, I would have said that some wars are necessary and justifiable. My views, however, were not the result of any careful self-examination. Now, when participation in one was a real possibility, I went back to my undergraduate habits: I needed to make my own personal, logical, and definitive determination, tied to my religious beliefs, of the question of whether war was ever justifiable.

My thinking was very much parallel to the rules of the draft. In order to be exempted from military service as a conscientious objector, one needs to object to all wars, not a particular war. At the time (and now), I think this is a reasonable position for the government. I believe that a democracy makes a reasonable compromise between individual liberty and the common good when it makes room for individuals who have a fundamental belief that violence should not be used to settle disputes, but does not allow individuals to pick and choose when they think the violence of war is appropriate. If selective objectors feel strongly enough about a particular war, they need to convince their fellow citizens to change the government and they may need to pay the cost of spending time in jail (I was impressed by Henry Thoreau's views on the time he spent in jail in objection to the Mexican-American war of the 1840s).

By the end of that year in Europe, I had convinced myself that no war was justifiable. Yes, I had considered World War II and found a way to fit even that "good war" into my scheme of thinking. Don't ask me to repeat my logic—as I said above, I see no point in trying to reconstruct a thirty-five-year-old thought process in an entirely different context. I am sure that I was not deceiving myself about my conclusions at that time. I wrote out my position to make sure all the logical points were covered. I forced myself to send this document to my father. I don't suppose that, even then, I thought he would understand, but I felt obligated to offer him an explanation for my decision.

Although I have not attempted to recapture and reevaluate my old arguments, I have spent a lot of time thinking about the context in which I came to my decision. That thinking, along with years of other experience, has taught me two lessons. In the world I lived in thirty-five years ago almost everything was black and white. I thought it was always possible to determine what was the right thing to do in any situation. Since "right" was always clearly distinguishable from "wrong," those who chose the "wrong" (Nixon) were clearly evil; those who chose the "right" (Eugene McCarthy) were clearly good. The first lesson I have learned is that we see the world through a murky glass. In particular, we can't always be sure about the consequences of our actions. Maybe those who choose a path I think is wrong simply analyze the consequences differently than I do. Maybe I should be looking for signs of intent and goodwill rather than outcomes that conform to my thinking. My lesson is not about moral relativism. I still believe absolute good and evil exist (Mother Teresa and Saddam Hussein). The problem is that most of us will never have a dramatic and clear-cut choice to make between good and evil. Following a moral path is a series of small choices for most of us, a matter of consistent commitment. Even when we are faced with a major choice, it is usually between "good" and "not so good" or "the lesser of two evils." We need to be prepared to admit that we will be wrong about some of those choices because we just couldn't see through the murk.

The second lesson is related to the first. If you want to answer for yourself an important, difficult and contentious issue, you will rarely (never?) get the right result by trying to figure it out on your own. You need to listen to people who disagree with you—and not just listen— you need to take their point of view seriously and assume that their good faith in addressing the issue may be equal to your own. This is a hard lesson to implement. No one, especially me, likes to listen to people who disagree with them about something important.

While I won't revisit my thirty-five-year-old decision, I have thought about the context in which I made it often enough for it to be a continuing source of discomfort. That discomfort will stay with me, as well as discomfort about whether I made the right moral choice many other times in my life. Neither confessing now to a old error or convincing myself I was right all along will make it go away.

The end to this story is that I notified the Army that I was a conscientious objector and wanted a transfer to the medical services corps; I wasn't trying to avoid being put in harm's way, and was ready to serve as a combat medic. I wanted to serve as a combat medic. The army chose to discharge me instead, as a reserve officer. I was still subject to the draft as an enlisted man and I was immediately drafted. I ended up serving two years of alternative service for a non-profit institution—hardly a great burden. From time to time I have to remind myself that I didn't run away from the war, but I did escape it, which often feels like the same thing.

Who Changed the Rules?

Sharon Fellows Larrison

Immersion back into the military life, after a few transitional years out, this time as the young bride of a Marine Corps 2nd Lieutenant, was natural and comfortable. Military bands on parade fields, with oh-so-proud Marines so full of hope and life, marching in unison, reinvoked our pride in being American.

A child of the 50s, taught to hide under my school desk during practice air raid drills because the communists might attack America, I was now caught up in the *domino theory* and fervently believed in the necessity of the war in Vietnam. Save Vietnam and we save the rest of the world from communism, or whatever. I was an easy sell. My goal now became to fully support my young Marine in his quest to get to Vietnam to save the country and the world. I embraced the *Esprit de Corps*, the propaganda, living and breathing in my belief in the righteousness of what we were doing. Young, strong, invincible; we are all so eager to go and to win. Until Terry R. died. One week into Vietnam, he stepped on a land mine, leaving a wife and two tiny children. The only one in our tightly knit group with children. In anguish and anger and shaken to the core, I cried and cried, absolutely shattered. This war was real. My Marine husband, appearing unaffected by the news, said, "Terry was stupid and got himself killed." I was horrified and uncomprehending of this attitude. Years later, upon reflection, I wondered if that had been his first step toward emotional disassociation in order to survive what was to come?

1968 brought the Tet offensive and my Marine began preparation to go to Vietnam. With mixed emotions, I, like many military wives, moved back home to my parents to wait out the 13 months until my Marine would come home. Days filled with work, with eager perusal of military newspaper obituary columns, scanning for the names of those I knew. There was almost always someone. Why were so many of my friends widows before the age of 24? Letters from Vietnam, with photos or slides, began morphing their way from optimistic love letters to letters with graphic details of jungle rot, rotting bodies, body bags and tools of torture... Tales of bounties on his head, silent moves in the night from village to village, psychological warfare in the guise of education and enlightenment, until, finally, a command of his own, in the jungle near Da Nang. Coping with my own fears, yet still supportive of our country's rationale to be in Vietnam, an ill-defined uneasiness began. Riots, public demonstrations and the burning of bras began in earnest demonstration against the war. My own sister, still living at home, joined the radical Students for a Democratic Society, in protest of the war. Within the walls of our parental home, the shouting matches between us were loud, heated and full of anger. How could she do this? Born and bred in a military family and married to an officer in Vietnam, for me to think of anything beyond support for the war was akin to treason of the heart, soul and family. I often wished I could flash back to chat with ancestors who lived and fought in the Civil War – brother against brother. How *did* the wives, mothers, and sister cope? Internal, personal confusion reigned.

As the months went by, the scenes of intense fighting in Vietnam became ordinary parts of the daily news, as did the increasing numbers of military personnel sent to Vietnam and the increasing numbers of those dying. My world became one of many military wives living near a base, hanging at the "O" Club for friendship from someone who understood. I volunteered and helped the military break the news of death and destruction to military wives, making necessary phone calls and holding the house together until distant family could arrive. I didn't last long. The raw grief and emotion was more than I could handle. I could barely cope with my own fears. The quiet conflict in my head continued. Something wasn't right. What *were* these guys dying for and when would it end? Wives of POWs, brainwashed by our government to believe they would soon bring their husbands home, suffered in silence, afraid to tip the balance and endanger the lives of their loved ones. After all, our military told them they would take care of them and of their husbands in captivity. *Good Girls Obey The Rules.*

The slaughter continued. Tradition and duty bound, we all remained silent. We had no role models for rebellion, or for higher aspirations, focused on self. Then one day, Jane Fonda sat on a cannon, igniting a shot heard round the world all over again. Call her traitor, or what you will, *someone had finally done something publicly and loud.* I saw Jane's actions as a catalyst for action. She set off a storm. POW wives began to unite and to raise their voices loudly and collectively to the stonewalling male military and within the halls of Congress and to the media. The public pressure intensified against the war. President Johnson decided he had enough and, in a dramatic announcement, decided not to run for a second term. Vietnam continued as a killer of men, and of careers.

The letters from my Marine in Vietnam became more sporadic, until no letters at all were forthcoming. Anxiety rose and an overwhelming dread became an all consuming part of every day. Then, the phone call in the hours just before dawn ended the suspense. "I've been wounded, I'm okay, and I'm in Okinawa now, not Vietnam." The military paid their obligatory call, with offers of assistance. Informed that I intended to go to Okinawa to see my husband, the Marine Corps met me with strong resistance. That old patronizing military mindset, "If We had wanted you to have a wife, We would have issued you one," was very much evident. Ever the child of my military upbringing, I knew my way around protocol and how to travel. *Good Girls Obey The Rules.* All the events and emotions of the past few years merged in my mind into one Eureka moment. I decided, "*Screw You.*" I'm not a *good girl* anymore. I got a passport, bought my own ticket, got my shots from the Air Force Base and took off for Okinawa. My astounded parents stood mute.

My Marine healed physically after a couple of surgeries and resigned his commission. The routine of life settled around us. We built a family and a business. Life was idyllic... or was it? Nightmares, night sweats, large glasses of scotch, withdrawing on an emotional level and acting out on a physical level became the norm about 10 years after Vietnam. Braggadocio surrounding no respect for authority or for rules. *"After all, what can they do to me? Send me back to Vietnam?"* Risk-taking, self-destruction in business, and in pleasure intensified. I thought my now ex-Marine was trying to kill himself. I learned later that he was.

A moment in time seared in my memory is a visual of me, standing in front of the television set, holding the vacuum cleaner, motor running, twelve or thirteen years after Vietnam. Dumbfounded, I stood in front of that TV, listening to a talk show discussion describing post-traumatic stress syndrome as it related to many Vietnam vets. They were describing my ex-Marine's behavior perfectly. A local vet center phone number appeared on the screen. At last, some understanding of what was happening to my ex-Marine and why. Survivor guilt, numbing shutdown of emotions. "If something were to happen to you and to the kids, that would be terrible, but I would be okay, it wouldn't really hurt," his echoing words as he tried to explain his inner self. Living with the ghosts of Vietnam is a hellish existence. Finally, and with relief, a divorce. Shattered dreams, fractured family.

Ghosts of wars past still remain, forever changing lives and relationships within families. My father, a WWII and Korean War veteran, fought those wars in his head and in his sleep and sometimes in public. He, and others I knew like him, drank to forget. Fathers of friends and relatives never reached their potential. Shattered dreams, tattered lives, fractured families, the legacy of war. Is it worth it? We willingly supported our government and our men. After all, *Good Girls Obeyed the Rules*. However, Vietnam became a wake up call. I struggled with the realization that our government lied to its citizens in it's zeal for *what* during Vietnam? False pride? Win at all costs? Today, with the wounds of Vietnam as fresh as 30 years ago, we

"JUST A LITTLE RAIN..."

still don't know how to answer the question why we were there and why we stayed so long. I do know, however, that Vietnam was a turning point in the fabric of life for American women. We learned we could step forward, at first tentatively and then often loudly, and truly make a difference in governmental policy, in personal lives and most importantly, we could and did reshape the *Rules*.

Ever a Don Quixote tilting in the wind, I continue to anguish over whether any battle is worth the price that I and so many others had paid. The personal sacrifices are so enormous and so irreparable, causing angst that flows from generation to generation in one form or another. As a mother, and now a grandmother to the next generation, potential battles become even more close and personal. No longer the young, naïve, rule-minding young woman, the thought of one of my own headed to battle is more painful than I could have ever imagined. Will I, however, step forward to stop another war, burn my bra in protest and vote for the potential pacifist? *No.* Having lived and traveled all over the world, I have experienced too much. Displaced Europeans living in camps 15 years after the end of World War II, citizens in foreign countries who take terrorism for granted and as an accepted part of life, numerous friends I made in Germany who lost a parent or a sibling while trying to scramble to freedom, into the West, and, most recently, the view from my seat on a Delta flight flying low over the burning Twin Towers in NYC on 9/11, and the trauma to my friends and to my country on that fateful day. I am grateful for the freedoms we have, and I more firmly tilt in the wind toward individual personal sacrifice, so that all may be free. It's a deep and personal choice, a choice that is made knowing that those of my now extended family and I could suffer indescribable pain and suffering. I have a choice, and I choose to stand for freedom of every kind, every place, no matter the sacrifice.

"Ask not what your country can do for you..."

Bob Flournoy, III

...during the last days of March, 1972, while Bill Clinton was in Moscow, our battalion found itself north of Saigon when the North Vietnamese launched their Easter Offensive, which would eventually end the war. We were part of the last combat ground forces left in country. The next 90 days would be full of uncertainty, and we would be serviced in the field marginally at best, as we patrolled the "rocket belt" (all points close enough to hit our major bases with big rockets). Our helicopter assets, the only way we traveled, were strained to the breaking point, supporting efforts to thwart the enemy's offensive just to our north at a place called An Loch. 40% of our aerial field artillery direct and general support would be lost in that engagement as those brave boys flying cobra gun ships engaged a totally unanticipated armor assault down that valley. One of the last futile gestures that registered a high cost in American blood.

By July, my brigade of the Cav was the last American combat unit in South Vietnam. Other than advisors to the South Vietnamese army, there were no other Americans in the bush. We were called the Gary Owen Task Force, and no one back home knew we were still out there trying to engage the enemy. I saw one soldier, a lieutenant, sit down on the landing zone outside of a firebase early one morning and,

"JUST A LITTLE RAIN..."

with weary rage, refused to get on a chopper that was taking our platoon on a combat assault. He had just read a newspaper article sent to him from his mother that claimed that there were absolutely no more American combat soldiers fighting in Vietnam. His resolve temporarily hesitated, but not his temper. The CO quietly spoke with him and reminded him of all that he would forfeit, all his bravery and all his sweat of the last 10 months, if he didn't just keep slogging ahead for a little while longer. He stood up and yelled at his platoon to quit gawking and get the hell rucked up and ready for the choppers. And away we went, into the cooling slipstreams of those fast Hueys as we sat in the doors and enjoyed the breeze, not knowing what awaited us. Not a word was ever spoken to that man by anyone ever about his 60 second breakdown. Respected by his men to begin with, I think that his short protest spoke for them all, and coming from an officer it had a welcome impact on them.

Days into that mission, I woke up one morning, deep in some remote jungle, with hepatitis and a fever of 103 and black urine. I stuck it out for a couple more days, until we were extracted for another insertion in another AO, but wound up in a field hospital, never to return to my unit. After two weeks, they stuck me on a medivac bird which made its way slowly back to the world with stops in the Phillipines, Guam and Hawaii. As sick as I was, I felt very guilty, because many of the men on that Air Force DC9 were shot up and burned pretty badly. I still do. As we sat on the runway in the dead of early morning night in Guam, the plane had its special medivac sides rolled up to allow for the transfer of liters, both on or off the aircraft. Air Force wives, living on the island with their husbands who were flying missions over North Vietnam, would come out to the medivac planes and sit with the sick and wounded, talking with them, bringing what comfort they could. I had my last glimpse of the war up close when one wonderful lady, who was sitting with me, looked up as a B52 roared down the runway just yards away from us, heading out on a mission. She must have recognized the tail number, because she crossed herself and said, "I love you, David," as it disappeared into the night.

I have tried for many years to mentally clarify the differences between my war and the wars of our fathers. WWI, possibly the most useless waste of life in history, was not glorified to my father's generation the way WWII was to mine. They were not exposed to television and movie glamorization of war as we were. When they did see a rare movie clip in a matinee, the figures jerked around like cartoon characters and wore funny looking hats. There was nothing to identify with, much less emulate. We lived WWII in real color, in your face heroism, almost daily. We stood in awe and unknowing jealous anticipation of an, as yet unidentified, opportunity so that we too could be a part of that brave brotherhood, and worthy. In Vietnam, we were all thankful that we were not fighting the surf invading Tarawa, freezing in France, or on the Yaloo River. Even in the midst of our own discomfort, we remained in awe of our fathers' exploits.

It is so difficult for so many reasons to draw comparisons between 'Nam and wars previously fought by American soldiers. The mindset of the country and the military was vastly different when we went into Vietnam from when we left over ten years later. Vietnam lasted three times as long as WWII and the combatants were much younger on average. We entered the war using WWII propeller-driven aircraft (A1 Sky Raiders) and wound up with aircraft that could touch the edge of space and travel at three times the speed of sound, so secret that they were just a rumor. We learned the horribly painful lesson that we could not fight in Vietnam like we had in Germany, Italy and Korea, and thousands of Americans died before our equipment and mindsets changed, and we began to fight the war as the tactical situation demanded, although the number of deaths did not abate.

The war in the swampy delta was vastly different from the war in the cold mountains of the north, along the DMZ, and each of those regions saw such an evolution of tactics, weaponry and engagement strategy by the enemy that 1965 only vaguely resembled what was happening in 1972. The war began with professional, highly motivated soldiers, national guardsmen and reservists, fighting a local guerilla army and ended with mostly reluctant draftees who did not have the resources to obtain deferments fighting professional soldiers from North Vietnam. These American kids were solid soldiers and continued to win in the field, but they did not represent the cross section of our society that has always been a hallmark of the

American fighting man. No small wonder that nothing has ever been written that has come close to capturing the entire mercurial Vietnam experience.

The war I watched develop on TV at the beginning of high school was still waiting for me when I got out of college, however, and many high school friends had died there by the time I commanded kids who were 8 or 9 years old when it started. It dominated a generation for over a decade, and the number of soldiers killed would have almost equaled that of WWII, had we not had such improved medical transportation assets on call. When the number of soldiers on the wall is counted, we forget that there were many more seriously wounded. When 500 Americans were dying a week during the late 1960s, another 3,000 were being wounded in the same time period. Nineteen-year-olds frequently spent a solid year in the jungle, banded together with 30 or more the same age, led by 22-year-old platoon leaders and 23-year-old company commanders, never knowing a break, just counting the days left that they had to survive.

Many left the bush on a Friday and were discharged onto the streets of Oakland or Newark within days. No 30-day ocean voyages to reflect on, no parades and brass bands, no cheering thanks from a grateful populace; no nothing. Typically, these kids had come from those same streets two years before, and they returned suddenly with some very unique skills and a sometimes ugly mindset to contribute to the old neighborhood. The much-talked-about post-traumatic stress, anger and confusion? Yes, for many, with very little direction on where they would go next, and certainly no help from the government. GI Bill? Many had not even graduated from high school, and college was never touted as an option in the young lives of those who did. That was such a vague aspiration that they did not even know to look in that direction. It is troubling to note that this was not an historical aberration. Discharged soldiers following the Civil War and WWI faced many of the same social reinstatement challenges, with a less than sympathetic government to help them return to their pre-war lives. Korean veterans returned to a society that was still basking in the glow of a WWII victory and faced, for the most part, a thankless homecoming. Only after WWII, it appears, was there an orderly assimilation of veterans back into the American landscape, and that was mostly due to the largess of the GI Bill, which addressed the government's fear of re-igniting the economic devastation of the depression by getting vets into school as opposed to seeing them all hit the job market at one time.

Shortly after I reported to my last duty assignment in Oklahoma, Richard Nixon, who had presided for four years over a war that he had inherited from two democratic administrations, was elected to a second term. His victory, over a candidate whose only platform was ending the war, was the biggest landslide in presidential election history. That overlooked fact seems hard to digest, looking back, but I guess that it makes the statement that the kids on campus and partying in the streets were not speaking for the American people. The North Vietnamese continued to use them and the media as powerful propaganda tools, and took heart that they were beating us at home, since they could not on the battlefield. Those protests by a very small portion of the American public, vastly exaggerated by the increasingly liberal media, prolonged the war and cost many lives on both sides by keeping our enemy away from inevitable peace negotiations.

It is interesting that when the draft was repealed, the protests stopped, even though American involvement in Vietnam would continue for over three more years. And, as the North Vietnamese butchered their brothers in the south after the war, there was not a peep from the sensitive, vociferous crowd that had supported the communists just a short time before. I often wonder where the protestors disappeared to over the last 30 years that have seen a unified Vietnam sink into a corrupt police state. I guess it was just about getting out, not about what was right any longer, as hard as that had become to define. I hold no animosity for those people, although their naïveté angered me, and I have a grudging respect for the few that just said "no" and presented themselves to the system for judgment, as opposed to those that ran north. Running grated on something deep inside of me, and still does. They may have been young and naïve, just like the those of us who went over, but the price that they must have paid since is surely depressingly heavy. Even now, I have little sympathy for them, although I know that is unhealthy. My door is wide open to those who remained firm on their convictions, however, and stood up to face the grating music of the time, either at home or "over there."

When my wife, Lorrie, and I took our ten-year-old son, Brent, to his first summer camp several years ago, we were shaken and fearful when we drove away and left him. His seven-year-old sister, Madison, was writing him a letter before we pulled out of the parking lot. Her little heart was already aching for him, as were ours. The week he was gone was an eternity of waiting and rampant imagining of what he must be going through. Only then, as a parent, could I understand what my own parents must have gone through daily while I was in 'Nam, or what my grandparents must have experienced while my dad and his two brothers were overseas in WWII.

As my son enters college on an ROTC scholarship, there are moments of black dread in me which literally jolt me awake in the middle of the night, as I wonder if he is doing the right thing. But, young men will always make their own decisions about such things, just as they have done for thousands of years. It is a matter of passion and adventure when it starts; blood up for the biggest ball game. The flag and patriotism are minor factors, having little to do with the initial motivation to go; it is something deeply ingrained in our genetic fabric.

Comparing Vietnam and the outbreak of WWII to the current war in Iraq is legitimate. Just like in 1941, we were attacked at home, on our own soil, with thousands of casualties. To say that there is more clarity of purpose now than in the early 1960s would be to forget the fervor with which we vowed to confront creeping communism, which had vowed to bury us, and which got us involved in 'Nam in the first place. There is the same initial sense of duty currently solidifying our military's commitment that there was forty years ago. But the confusion, frustration and regret that linger from unresolved issues in Vietnam still haunts us—the meaning of it all, elusive.

Political opponents of our war against terror, regrettably, will continue to play the Vietnam card, and use those lingering doubts to their advantage, out of selfish spite or downright ignorance. I do pray that the current conflict does not bog us down for another decade or more of divisive unrest, but I fear that it will, as the years go by and our moral resolve and response to the outrage of 9/11 fades from our collective memory. This conflict, too, may be impossible to bring to a decisive end, even though we will continue to win militarily, just like we did in Vietnam. Our decision to go into Vietnam was not a poor moral choice, it was a poor tactical choice. It was always the enemy's field and their time; we never had a chance long term. Vietnam was the wrong place to make a stand, due strictly to the geographical exigencies that it presented. Isolated in a hostile environment with a thousand miles of indefensible borders, there was never a possibility to bring about a conclusive ending. Unlike the French, who were beaten on the battlefield, we just got tired, and left, betraying the people who had come to depend on us; an offense that we were to repeat in 1992 in another war.

We must carefully pick our battlefields in the war that we are now engaged in to prevent the same type of endless predicament. I fear that the unseen wounds still bleeding from Vietnam will agitate the souls of the current combatants in a similar fashion with time, and as years accumulate and we settle into this religious war on terror, we may be doomed to settle for the same indecisive conclusion, unable in our lifetime to declare victory, unable to walk away like we did in Vietnam.

Already we are seeing Vietnam-type politically motivated decisions being made in Washington that tie the hands of our military leaders and cost American lives, portending the same hazy outcome that we had in 1975. Time may again be on the side of our enemy as they let our system eat away at itself from the inside. There is more at stake today, however, and the global battlefield may require that we act more decisively than at any other time in our history. If there is even a hint that our enemy has the capacity to strike a telling blow against us, and we do not pre-emptively take them out, it can truly mean our end.

All that having been said, I would do it again in a heartbeat. As a boy, I had a tendency to choose friends based on how they measured up to the expectations and points of integrity that my father had instilled in me. I found a few who served and some who did not, who met those standards, and I guess some of them found it in me, but I owe the Army and the whole 'Nam thing for many of those guys, and

"JUST A LITTLE RAIN..."

a sense of myself that I would not have otherwise. That is just the way it is, and while the nation paid a steep price for such a right of passage, it is my not-uncommon story, still somewhat confused after all these years, just like that era itself.

My thoughts and opinions are not judgments, and I am still wide open to someone—anyone—giving me anything that I can use to see the whole affair more clearly. The rambling attempt in these pages to put Vietnam into focus speaks, as I intend it to, to the futility of coming to very many concrete conclusions. It will probably require that we all die and let agenda history have its way with the whole issue, encapsulating it into a three volume set where academics can pontificate on "what we did wrong," before there is closure.

It is surely easier to write about history with all of the conveniences of hindsight. The mass of writings that reflect other people's thoughts are at your disposal, and they have contributed subconsciously to your own ideas that you might think are original. It is a much more daunting task to place yourself in those past moments as though you are in the present time, unfettering your thoughts with historical prejudice, making those decisions that were made then, yourself. It is a near impossible task, so strong are the temptations to assume a wiser stance, secretly armed with your future knowledge.

Bob Flournoy, June 1972

State of Mind

Bob Flournoy

When the blackness arrives, it is just there. There is no dusk or twilight, just a sudden nauseating midnight. If you've been in this place before, then it scares you when it first announces its return, because you know what it has in mind for you and you don't know if it is here to stay, or if it is just going to play around with you for a little while. I wonder if you have to come up out of the pain at its first glint and just raged against it. Maybe that is an initial affective anticdote; if acts of defiance prevent it from establishing a beach head, or if concessions and appeasement make the looming battle more difficult. Maybe it will just go away by itself later in the day, like a short virus, regardless of how you confront it. An extended fight might just kill me the next time. I have no heart for it, now that I know the brutality of such terror. Hell, perhaps I'll just clean the garage in a frenzy, furiously lift weights like a young man, run farther faster than my age can withstand for very long, talk too loud, and drink way too much with a forced bravado and energy, a bonfire with loud drums and spear brandishing against the night. I'll paint my face and turn to the forest, my back to the flames, plain to see, screaming for a head-on confrontation to kill the beast. Come on you son of a bitch, I'm right here where you can see me and I am ready for you. But the buzzard just sits out there silently, lurking, waiting; the stink of his breath teasing the tepid air, sensing your fear and knowing that you must come looking.

Flashback

Bob Flournoy, III

...walking out your patio door on a very hot summer day when the heat hits you like a hot wet towel and hearing, simultaneously, the sound of your six-year-old son popping caps on the cement with a rock as a HUEY happens to be flying over leaving you dizzy, disoriented and slightly sick to your stomach, sad and in the dumps for the rest of the day...

Moving On

Bob Flournoy, III

Texas became a memory as I grew and traveled the world with my family and later by myself. I met, loved and left people in that sort of nomadic lifestyle that military families endure, but never forgetting them—any of them. When I left for Vietnam, the most common words that people spoke to me were, "We will pray for you." I never knew what to say, knowing that these were reflex words that people uttered when they meant something much more heartfelt, but lacked the comfort or ability to express. I politely thanked them for their thoughts, without attaching too much literal meaning to them. I was caught up in the events of the moment and was not concerned about events to come. And, of course, it would never be my neck that fate got its hands around.

I was spiritually content and respectful of the universal moral teachings of Jesus and others in the course of human history who have stood up for what they believed to be right (all a given in my family). I pursued my awe of the concept of God the Creator, the force that defined everything outside the restraints and confines of the Christian church. The not-so-carefully crafted religions of the world held no interest for me after I had examined and even lived a few of them. They challenged me as I sifted through them, trying to make sense of my Christian upbringing, and I tried to find some religious ideas that fit my experience of the world. I knew that the soul journeys on after death, having witnessed it first hand, so I quietly slipped away from the confusion of a theology that demanded obedience to its decrees of how God should be viewed. I knew that the ominous words blasphemy and heresy were expressions invented by the church to protect itself from inquiry. I found that all religions, with their myths and suppressing dogmas, conflicted with my own common sense, studied deliberation and conclusions.

It is a hard thing for people in our culture to ask themselves if Christianity really speaks for Jesus, and if the church has a clue as to how to go about grappling with the notion of a creator that does not center his energies around this little blip in the continuum called "man." I wondered what would happen to our lofty religious musings when we joined the list of a billion species that have already gone extinct in the split second of time that life itself has been on the landscape. God makes sense, and I pursued Him from that foundation. We may not understand many of the things that we refer to as supernatural, but that does not mean that they are not a part of the grand scheme of things, and are ultimately as natural as the mysteries of the universe that we have already unraveled.

A fundamental part of my belief was that the notion of a god that needs to be worshipped, judges, and punishes was absurd and offensive. I vowed never to let anyone ever tell my children that they were sinners who needed saving from the spirit that they were born with. I had a big problem with the basic tenant of Christianity that preached forgiveness as a bedrock of the religion. Admittedly, imperfect man needs to feel forgiven by his fellow man from time to time as a reassurance that all is well, but to assign this attribute to God did not compute. An uninterrupted flow of divine love does not recognize the need to pause and make a gesture of forgiveness. Just as our love for our own children is pure and unbroken, negating the need to make such a gesture, so must be the love of God. That basic misunderstanding of love, the attachment of conditions, might have translated to a workable religion that attempted to exert influence and control over an emerging, uneducated civilization so many years ago, but it is not good theology, and it desecrates the very concept of real love that it claims as its own.

I found the historical debris of monotonous liturgy and changing dogma that the centuries had strewn in the path of those seeking God to be confusing obstacles in a quest which should be simple. I threw that great mass of obstruction aside so that I could just close my eyes and try for a glimpse of the Man (I use that description for brevity) himself, without the centuries of chaotic thunder that had been accumulating in my mind. I knew that many people could sit in the congregation on Sunday morning and listen passively, even emotionally, to the preaching that changes very little from Sunday to Sunday, year to year, and I did not question their need to do that, but I could not. The staggering concept of God deserved more intellectual honesty and truth. I knew that I, personally, could not reconcile a blind call to religious obedience with my need to search open-mindedly.

But, when the time came that so many I knew and loved were dying I cast about for comfort; a lonely emotional quest, helped little by my new found, somewhat isolated, spiritual self. I tried to remember that the universe that we are a part of is timeless and that it is unfolding as it should be, too vast to capture in even our most expanded imagination. I knew this pain of loss was not personal, it was just the way it was, and that we had been gifted and challenged with the unique ability to try and make sense of it all, if only as tiny specs of energy in the infinite timeline of a borderless cosmos. I was searching for a glimpse of the truth, and when it was revealed, I was overwhelmed by the sense of peace and contentment which it brought, and still provides. The sign was clear and unmistakable...

All I'll Ever Need

Bob Flournoy, III

There was a shrub outside the kitchen window of my grandparent's isolated farmhouse in rural Alabama, and my grandmother used to talk to the mockingbirds just inches away through the glass panes as she performed her various chores at that old sink. I can still see and hear her standing there talking to those birds like they were small children. They flitted in and out of the bush, seemingly oblivious to her, squawking and making the racket that mockingbirds are known for. She died when I was overseas in the Army. My aunt (Dad's sister-in-law) lived in town nearby and went out and cleaned and straightened up the old house when she passed away. Many years later, when we were spending some time together doing what I do not remember, she got a faraway look in her eyes and asked if she had ever told me about cleaning the stuff out of my grandmother's bedroom a couple of days after she had died. I said no, and she said that the strangest thing had happened. One mockingbird had beat its wings against the bedroom window and made a tremendous amount of noise, like it wanted inside with my aunt as she cleaned out dresser drawers and so forth. Merle, my aunt, said it was almost as if that bird were desperately trying to communicate with her. She had never seen anything like it and it made an impression on her, obviously, for her to bring it up to me after so much time had elapsed.

Years later, as my mom was fighting cancer, I read everything I could find on the subject of her disease. One of the best books I read was by a doctor who had seen much death in his career and had witnessed some unexplainable events associated with the various deaths that he had been exposed to. One of the events, that caught my eye because of my aunt's experience with the mockingbird, was this doctor's recounting of the death of one of his patients who was also his good friend. The doctor went out jogging one morning before he went to visit his buddy in the hospital, and a black bird started flying parallel to him, singing. As he ran, the bird kept pace and then flew away. He knew beyond a doubt that his friend had died and that his soul was communicating with him through the unusual behavior of this bird. He went to the hospital immediately and, sadly, his friend had passed away during those moments when this bird had sought him out.

The day came when my sisters and I sat on my mom's bed with her and held her as she painfully passed away. Just before she became quiet I whispered in her ear to send us a sign that she was okay. My exact words were, "Send us a little bird, Mom, to let us know that all is well." We were all very emotional, of course, but my words were witnessed by both of my sisters. My spontaneous request of her in her last seconds was driven by not only heartbreaking desperation, but with the memory of what my aunt and the doctor had been confronted with in their own experience.

My sisters and I had all flown in to Hampton to be with my mom and were all staying in her little house. We spent the next day doing that most painful of things, putting away her stuff and dealing with the bittersweet memories. That afternoon, as I was doing something in one of the bedrooms, I heard my sisters start to scream and cry for me. I went running through the kitchen to see them sitting and hugging each other on the steps leading down out of the kitchen into the garage. Unable to say anything they pointed to the middle of the garage floor where a small bird sat looking at us and chirping. We sat and watched it for awhile and it hopped out of the garage and into the bushes, gone. I went out a moment later to look for it, but I could not find it.

There is no doubt what happened there to us on that day; not a one. I believe we all get similar signs in our lives, but we have been numbed to their appearances and we do not see them through the noise and confusion of the way we live in these times. Our instincts to recognize such contacts have long since atrophied. My son and I had a similar experience when my father-in-law passed away. He sent us a sign, loud and clear, and we both recognized it instantly. It was the most extraordinary thing that could possibly have happened to him (my son), because now he knows, believes, and is vigilant to the vague but meaningful phenomena in his life that most people do not ever see.

Just because we don't understand things doesn't mean they aren't part of something large and true. The years have made me a very pragmatic realist who deals with the world as it is presented everyday. But I have seen the souls of my loved ones as they began a new journey. That experience makes me smile, and the romantic child who once believed in magic is reassured that mystical meaning and grace, although elusive, are still with us, auras of beauty that envelope the heart of our very existence.

A Continuous Quest

Bob Flournoy

If we are the products of evolution and natural selection, which we certainly are, I wonder when our souls showed up on the time line. Have they been waiting for us through the eons, looking for a place to roost, or were they endowed in a display of largess and love by a power who glanced our way in the vastness of the cosmos, and said, "Wow, look what happened over there"? Did the concept of love exist before the evolution of mankind's ability to feel it? Is human love an evolutionary extension of a lesser animal's short-lived concern for its offspring?

My challenge has been to find people who can consider the concept of God outside the realm of organized religion and restraining theology, with no preconceived opinions that have been planted culturally. I mean, try challenging a member of the Christian clergy to a discussion about God which forbids any reference to the bible or any other teachings of that religion and you are going to have a very strained conversation. The idea that mankind is the center of the universe and that God's main mission focuses on human beings is so ingrained in most of us that it is hard to kick up a good discussion of man's place in a cosmos where billions of light years and an equal number of galaxies are the parameters. In a recent dinner conversation with a friend and minister of an evangelical church, my opening statement that life on earth began as we sat down to the first course and will end before the dessert, left him blank and disoriented. Not so much that he could not grasp the concept as he had spent not a single minute in his own life preparing him for such a discussion. So, when someone tells me that they are seeking God, I assume that they are studying physics and chemistry to augment their spiritual quest. I mean, really, how can you set your sights on a *creator* if you don't have a rudimentary understanding of His tools? Sadly, some early contributors to the bible, realizing that man's instincts are to imagine and dream, and fearful that many of their ideas would be exposed for their lack of truth, taught that questioning these narrow minded viewpoints was sinful, thereby eroding the many powerful and beautiful words to be found in the rest of the book. I am constantly amazed at the self-imposed intellectual boundaries that so many Christians adopt out of fear that their very thoughts might violate the edicts of those early biblical authors who believed that the sun orbitted an earth that was flat. And, what kind of twisted thought process imagined and ingrained into its religion the concept of something so evil as hell, instilling that threat into their childrens' heads at the same time they were talking about God's love?

And I Still Remember Tony ...

Bob Flournoy, III

I first met Tony Mintino when we lined up side by side that first day of basic training at Ft. Benning, so very long ago in the humid furnace heat of south Georgia in July. I took an immediate dislike to him because he was from New Jersey and talked a lot about baseball. Everyone knew that only southerners played good baseball. Didn't they? I had temporarily forgotten Dimaggio, Ruth, Berra, and Gehrig. You know, those guys from New York. I was not to know for twenty years that Tony had died later on some forgotten landing zone near the Cambodian border, trying to use the skills that we were about to learn en route to a close friendship. He was from New Jersey and was studying American Literature at Columbia University, with an emphasis on Faulkner. He knew everything about William Faulkner, you see, even if he had never been in the deep south until this "visit," and he pontificated loftily with a degree of Yankee arrogance on our culture and its influences on one of our most celebrated southern sons. I took up the challenge to educate my new pal and enhance his understanding of this man, Faulkner, motivated by some combative perversity that was to mellow over the next eight weeks and grow into a grudging admiration for his willingness to be educated by a good-old-boy from *down here*. His open mindedness and sincere interest in my southern perspective captured my heart and became the basis for our friendship and my own learning experience about his particular culture and life. He later wrote to me that he had started a manuscript from the notes that he made from the memory of our many conversations in the field and that they would be the basis for his graduate thesis after he left the Army and returned to New York.

"Tony, if you have never sat on a Mississippi porch of a farmhouse that borders a dirt road twenty miles from anything at midnight in August with the bugs thick in your dripping sweat and the frogs booming from the swamp while your great grandmother spoke in barely a whisper about the union troops that had burned her house and the chaos of reconstruction that tore the land apart worse than the Civil War itself did, then you cannot know Faulkner. You cannot know a thing about the causes of the anguish and passion in the soul that wrote about the brooding pains of his native land."

And so I began to talk about my own unfulfilled loves, passions and haunted dreams and the elusive tone of a land whose memories were slowly being washed away by the winds of time and agenda history. We talked for the eight weeks that we were together about our lives and families, and I believe that we both came away with an understanding of the similarities that our different backgrounds bore.

I had grown up all over the world with my military family as my father rotated between duty assignments. Personally, the rewards of this life had been many, to include a sense of geography, cultures and the history and language associated with each relocation. My family moved eight times before my sixteenth birthday. No matter how far away we were, however, we made that trek to my grandparent's Alabama farm on an annual basis, to keep a sense of place and home burning brightly in our hearts and minds. The anticipation of these visits, fueled by the memories of past trips, caused an imprint of every moment of the actual visit in my mind that remains with me these many decades later. No matter where I was living, I knew that I was a southerner with ancestors and roots so deep and tangled that I was part of something huge. And, as I compared what I learned about my people and their lives, I developed a strong sense of pride as I realized that they measure up to all of the people and places I was being presented with around the world. I liked to think Tony responded to my passion and that it touched something in his hot Italian blood, and maybe because it had been missing in his own life. His unselfish ability to listen caused me to reflect many years later that I should have done more listening, myself, about his story and people.

When we got our first weekend off from basic, Tony and I hitchhiked 40 miles from Fort Benning to my grandparent's farm west of Columbus, Georgia, just into Alabama. We were 20 years old, in uniform, and very proud. Who could have known the rigors of our previous weeks and the sense of superiority and accomplishment that it had been instilled in our young hearts? My grandparents greeted us with warmth and food, both of which had been absent in our previous six weeks. Here was an Italian Jew sitting in the farmhouse of old southern people born before 1900 gaining their respect and love with his quiet dignity and amazement at just being there. What must my grandmother have been thinking, having seen three sons off to World War II just 23 years before? I am sure that she saw them sitting before her, once again, us having no clue what awaited us, or what she must have endured while they were gone.

Tony and I spoke once on the phone after basic, and bumped into each other in the bar of the officers' club in Ft. Benning, quite by accident. We had both returned from our branch basic courses for paratrooper training and were feeling pretty good about those new wings on our chests, back when jump school meant something. I eventually wound up in the central highlands of Vietnam as an artillery forward observer with an infantry unit in the First Cavalry Division, and I had one note from Tony telling me that he was a platoon leader with the 101st Airborne, far to the north near the DMZ, which was very bad country. I then lost contact with Tony, but I made many other friends that only come to you in the Army during wartime, and my life went forward after Vietnam and the military. I thought about Tony occasionally; I thought about a lot of people whom I had known during my three years of duty, but youth drove me on, with 'Nam becoming a fading memory. My grandparents would always ask about him when I saw them; before I lost them, too. My granddad would smile and ask me whatever happened to that "Eye-talian Yank."

In 1987, I was visiting Birmingham, Alabama, and I ran into an old ROTC college buddy on the street in broad daylight. Like I had seen him just last week on campus, I greeted him and we caught up with each other's lives. I learned that he had served in the 101st during Tony's tour and casually asked if he recognized the name. As those things so often happen, he had served in the same rifle company with Tony, also as a platoon leader, and that is where I learned Tony's fate; killed on a hot LZ in some remote valley north of Phu Bai. I bade farewell to my old college acquaintance and wandered abstractly around my father's hometown for about an hour, trying come to grips with what I had just been told. I never did, and still have not. I have never made any sense of any of it. There were hundreds of Mintinos in the New Jersey phone directory, and I never found his family.

I visited my old school, Auburn, not too long ago on a trip through Alabama, and I took a solitary drive out to my grandparent's old place. I have done that many times in my adult life. I think I am trying to put something in its proper place, to assign an order to those days, so that the memories there can be put to bed. Looking back, I can see the book in its entirety, I just can't focus on the chapters, much less the words. We all die, I think, wishing that we had left things a little more in order, and I think we are mostly tired when that time finally comes, having tried to sort out the poignant places and events in our pasts so that our hearts can rest. But, those defining moments from our youth call to us across the years, no matter how old we become. The old farm had changed a lot since my last visit. The fields were green with grass instead of crops, and the house had been completely redone. The orchards were gone and so was the cotton.

Dismayed, yet not surprised, that nothing was as I remembered it to be, I pulled down the little dirt road that ran beside the property. I sat and stared out across the empty fields of my grandfather's farm and I tried to focus on all of the people in my life that I had known and loved. I thought about Tony and his animated face as he watched my grandfather make buttermilk biscuits on the old iron stove. I tried to remember all of the lost faces and their distant voices as it started to gently rain. I got out of the car, strangely comforted by the distant soft, crumping rumble of friendly thunder impacting in the distance. I walked into the field that I had been in so long ago, and I turned my face into that soft sweet sky. As the rain began to soak into my skin, I opened my mouth to scream into the heavens, appealing to all those whom I had lost. But instead, I just closed my eyes and started praying, out loud, trying to drown out the rising wind and wet warm drops, thanking God, finally after all these years, for the beautiful rain in this special place that my grandfather had asked for. What else could I do?

The short drive down the old dirt road to the tiny country church that I had attended with my grandparents as a child was rewarded with open doors and no one present, and I found that the modest interior had changed little in the almost 50 years since I had last been there. Softly lit by the slanting sun coming in through the modestly colored windows, I sat in the last row of hand-hewn, decades-old pine pews, next to my departed family, and remembered their sweet, innocent, hopeful voices singing the once again familiar hymns whose words rang clearly in my head after all this time. I focused on each individual voice, one at a time. I saw their expectant faces turned to me, and I knew that I was home.

Final Thoughts

Grandparents, home towns, childhood and military friends, gone or gone their own way, but never forgotten. Like the crack of a bat and the smack of a mitt, which were the piper's call to a game for generations of boys who were caught up in the siren's song of baseball. We have been trying to recapture the definitive moments in our pasts ever since it became the past, and we began looking back, wistfully wondering where it went. Was it Fitzgerald who told us that we do not look back, searching for events, we merely search for our youth? If you didn't cry, or at least get choked up, when a son and his dead father played catch in "Field of Dreams," then you have lost the magic. But, I bet you had it once, just like all the rest of us did. We may have filed the unpleasant things in our lives off in some corner of our minds, but not baseball. We are still waiting for that perfect pitch. And just when the curtain is falling, we'll be wanting one more at bat, one more race down the base path, one more real game.

Bob Flournoy, III

Grandad Flournoy Making Biscuits

My River

Bob Flournoy - June 2004

When I was young
my spring water sparkled and danced in the sun
and the stones in my bed were bright and polished.
I fell haphazardly forward, bounding downward,
inertia propelling me on gravity's course, forward
toward the murky mouth and inevitable slow tug
of my waiting river.

I am broad and sweeping now, a creeping expanse
embracing companions of moss and debris,
inching onward,
languidly searching
for the tranquil lower ground
and the endless expanse of the deep sea.

Remembered

Brent Cameron
Jon Shine
Terry Ranstead
Steve Matthews
Bronson Westfall
Bryan Tibbett
Kirk Thompson
Alex Boyd Conley
Terrell Blalock
Johnny Weger
Denny Vaughan
Paul Murray
Archie Sutterer
Bruce Edmonds
Art Parker
Barry Kerr
Guy Hester
Jim Dugger
Tom Brennan
Terry O'Boyle
Ken Cummings

…And so many more…

Last Thoughts

Since finishing the original manuscript, *"Just a Little Rain,"* several months ago, the world has become a place even more ominous than I had feared at that time. The quagmire in Iraq has worsened, forcasting an unwinnable scenario that will surely engulf the entire region, as the spectre of Iranian nuclear weapons has reared its head. That, coupled with the seepage of poorly controlled nuclear material from the former Soviet Union, the threatened government of nuclear capable Pakistan, and the inevitable military involvement of Israel as the conflict escalates, paints a potential, no, a probable doomsday scenario for the near future. The average citizen of this country does not perceive the brink of almost unavoidable disaster that we teeter on. My son is home from college, and I have requested that he read *Flyboys,* the greatest book that I have ever read, which addresses the willingness of mankind to slaughter his fellow human beings. I have also presented him with Ray Hill's thoughts, which are present in my book, and why, in light of what happened then and what is occuring now, I have such respect for that kind of thinking so long ago. And finally, I have asked him to consider, very carefully, as an ROTC scholarship cadet, his own personal involvement in the events that will envelop him in the years to come. I know what his decision will be. Mine would probably be the same. There is, however, a sadness and dread in my heart that I cannot abate. I hope I am wrong, but I know that I am not.

Bob Flournoy
November 22, 2004

About the Author

Bob Flournoy lives in Franklin, Tenn., with his wife Lorrie and two children: Brent, 19, and Madison, 16. He is a professional artist, and although he has begun writing only recently, he is working on his next book, calling on many experiences of a rich and diverse life to define its course.

Printed in the United States
69803LV00001B/52-69